THE
CONCEPTION OF
UTOPIA

THE
CONCEPTION OF
UTOPIA

One Woman's Journey
into New Shamanism

CHERIZAR WALKER

**TURNING
STONE
PRESS**

Cover design by Frame25 Productions
Print book interior design by Frame25 Productions

Turning Stone Press
San Antonio, TX
www.turningstonepress.com

If you are unable to order this book from your local bookseller, you may order directly from the publisher.

ISBN: 978-1-61852-138-5

10 9 8 7 6 5 4 3 2 1

For Hugo.

I wrote this book so you will know
how much love brought you into the world.

What is that feeling when you're driving away from people and they recede on the plain till you see their specks dispersing?—it's the too-huge world vaulting us, and it's good-bye. But we lean forward to the next crazy venture beneath the skies.

—Jack Kerouac, *On the Road*

Contents

The History of the Future

I would say that my story starts with death.

My brother Yannick was riding his bike, and my friend Lindsay, who weighed more than him, was on the handlebars. I remember thinking that this wasn't the brightest idea considering we were on a very steep hill. And I was right because the next thing I knew, I saw Yannick doing a front flip over the handlebars and come crashing down onto the asphalt. I ran to him frantically and saw his wrist bone sticking out of the skin. He was just sitting there, staring at it. I started to walk backwards, feeling as if the wind had been knocked out of me. I just felt so afraid for him, and the broken bone was more than my eyes could handle.

That was back in middle school when my older brother was too cool for me. But as we got older, we started to get closer. When I was in the eleventh grade, we lived about fifteen miles from my high school, so he would come pick me up in his red Bronco, music blaring, and with his sunglasses facing the wrong way. There were certain songs that he would play repeatedly: "Hotel California" by the Eagles, "Regulate" by Nate Dogg and Warren G, a plethora of Pennywise and Tupac songs, and this song called "Freshman" by The Verve Pipe that I just heard the other day.

When the melody hit my ear, a rush of memories of my brother came with it. It was as if part of his spirit was carried in the melody, and the song hit me in the stomach like it did seeing him break his arm so long ago. After I listened to it, I played it again; and then I played it again and again.

As I cried, I could see him listening too. I could see him listening to it as he worked on his truck, mouthing every word of the song. The song is about the undying, stubborn youth inside of us. And it's fitting because in some way I will always see Yannick through the lens of this song—so recklessly alive, so recklessly free.

The waves of grief that wash over me make me wonder what this song meant to him, because now it means so much to me. I listen to it when I drive, and I imagine him on the other side, as my passenger.

When I heard the news, everything inside of me told me it couldn't be true, that he couldn't be dead. His funeral was an open casket, and I didn't dare look. I am quite sure I don't believe in that, but to have the last image of him be that—I couldn't bring myself to do it. I watched from afar in shock, still not believing.

And even now, years later, it's still hard to believe. Sometimes, I just think that it's been a while since I've seen him.

On the day he was killed though, I found something that I didn't know I had. I found these two voicemails from him. One of them congratulates me on the birth of my son, and the other wishes me a happy Thanksgiving. I listen to them from time to time, to recall through his voice how sweet he was. And how, in spite of what he wasn't telling me, there was still a part of him in need of our connection.

There's another voicemail that I still have, and that I'll never delete. This one is from my mom. At the time, she was in the desert with no service, and I was the first person to get ahold of her to tell her what had happened to him. I can't remember exactly what I said, but it was almost like she knew what I was going to say before I said it. The call dropped soon after, and she tried to call me back but couldn't reach me, so she left me a voicemail. In the message, she lets out a scream so horrible that I wouldn't wish it on my worst enemy to hear. It's the most heartbreaking moment I've ever witnessed that I only heard. I had seen my mom lose her sister, and she cried like a baby, like a little girl, but this cry carried with it a crippling pain. I don't know why, but I still listen to it sometimes. I guess I don't ever want to forget what true pain sounds like.

My story starts with death because it was the coldness of death that painted the warmest picture of life. It was in the contrast where I found the infinitude of love that I never knew was inside of me. All this love I found, hiding inside of me.

Three years have passed since my brother's death, and I feel I've begun to live a life more meaningful. A lot has shifted in my life since I made acquaintance with death. So much so that I find myself somewhere I never thought I would be—on the doorstep of the house of the man who is meant to be my guide. His name is Paul, and he is a medium. I don't know what he is meant to tell me, but I know that I am meant to ask him why I'm being called to the center of the Earth. For the past month, I've had this feeling that I'm meant to study with the shamans of Ecuador. I heard about this retreat, and I just can't get it out of my heart, and I don't understand why. I've always been intrigued by shamanism, but there was nothing I had ever done that would lead me to believe that I was meant for something of this magnitude. Something inside of me had already committed to going, though. I had already decided that it was written in the stars, but I just needed to know why. I needed Paul to tell me who I was becoming and what reality I had awoken to.

The sun was just beginning to set as I watched Paul walk up the steps to greet me. He looked like a normal guy; not sure what I expected. The feeling of being an observer in my own life overtook me and carried me down the stairs. Everything seemed to be an abnormality cloaked in normality. Paul led me to what looked like a greenhouse; inside, I could tell it was his office. The images on his walls and those that came to mind as I sat in the room made me aware of his expertise as an energy practitioner. He is a very gifted man. I wonder what life is like on the edge of the supernatural.

He explained to me that he would pass on the messages from my spirit guides. He closed his eyes, and it seemed as if he was downloading information. He was sitting at his desk, and I was facing him, watching intently, wondering what words he would absorb from the sky. After a few seconds, he opened his eyes and took a deep breath. The words came out faster than he could say them: "Ninety percent of what you will experience in this life is a result of your past lives.

One of the things that you must learn in this life, one of your karmic lessons, is to delegate and to let go of control. And that's what you did in your last relationship, so congratulations. Your ex-husband had been your ex-husband for three lives, this is the fourth. This is the first time in many lives you walked away from him. Because for many lives you didn't, and you lost your life because of it. He would have killed you."

I interrupted him because I couldn't believe what he'd just said. Sure, things had gotten pretty bad in the end of my marriage to my ex, Bruno, but: "Wait. What? He would have literally killed me?!!"

"Yes. He flips out. This is his tendency based on his past life experiences."

I nodded my head in agreement. "Well, he did have his moments, just like we all do. But it's still hard for me to grasp all of this though. It seems both believable and not. I feel now though, that because I left him, he was set free from this cycle. That we were both set free from the karmic energy that bound us."

"Yes, that's exactly right."

Bruno and I had officially broken up about six months ago, and immediately afterward, I felt as if a weight had been lifted off both of our shoulders. Our love was a burden that neither of us could bear anymore.

We cried about it and expressed to each other our gratitude. It was a beautiful breakup.

Paul didn't take even a moment to pause in between his revelations.

"Your aura is purple, and that's why people gravitate towards you. You have a protective, motherly energy that people are attracted to. You were a scribe in a past life. Your guides speak to you through your writing and provide many of your intuitive ideas. You need to meditate though, to organize all of this. You are very scatterbrained and are unable to focus on bringing these ideas to completion."

"Yes . . . unfortunately, this is true."

"In a past life, your son Hugo was a gangster. He was a boss in the South American cartel. That's why he speaks the way he does. He makes commands, right?"

"Yes. He says, 'Give me this' and 'give me that,' even though he has never heard any of us speak like that. It's crazy."

"Yes, it's his past life coming through. He chose you as his mother so you could show him the power of feminine energy. He is very masculine. . . . Your guides are telling me that you are distant from your family. Is this true?"

"Well, they live far away, but I would say we are as close as we could be. Something happened to our family that was tragic and left us scarred. My brother Yannick was murdered."

"I'm sorry to hear this."

"Yeah, I still can't believe it. There is, like, a reality I can go to where it didn't happen, and he's here with me. And what's even weirder than that is the last time I saw him, I knew it would be the last time. I could like sense Death stalking him. I thought I was nuts. But in the end, it was true. It was our last time together."

Paul paused and seemed to pick up on something else, something different. "Your brother is here. He too was a gangster in a past life.

In the same life as Hugo, they were father and son. All of our family and closest friends in this life were people we were also close to in past lives. So the way your brother acted was because of his gangster past life. He was trying to be someone he wasn't. He is talking to me now: He says that he is sorry. He is sorry that he couldn't be the brother you could look up to. He wished he would have been more like you and that he is happy to able to speak to you. He is talking about drawing or something. Was he an artist?"

"Yes, he was a really good artist."

Hugo has this same talent, and there are times when I feel Yannick watching me through Hugo, like they're deeply connected. This past-life situation explains it. They met only once when Hugo was seven months old, but they had this instant bond. Yannick had driven across town in heavy LA traffic to see us before we left to go back home to Montréal. We hung out for a while, and before I left, I got the strangest feeling that it would be the last time I would see him. I remember thinking that I was being crazy or something, but the feeling of death watching him was undeniable. That night was the last time I saw Yannick.

"Okay, yes, he is saying that he could have been a tattoo artist if it wasn't for those damn pills. I guess it was the pills he was addicted to. He realizes now that he let a lot of people down. He is showing me a car. I think he was doing chop-shop type of work."

"Probably. He was an amazing mechanic. My dad actually did that kind of stuff too when he was a kid. Crazy."

"He is playing Tupac in the background."

"Yes, he loved Tupac." My tears turned to laughter as I thought about how he used to listen to Tupac all the time. He would always play that album *Better Dayz*.

"The reason I listen to Tupac now is because of him."

"Oh yeah? He says that he got to meet Tupac."

"Of course he did. What a life." I laughed to know that Yannick was happy in the afterlife at Thugz Mansion. I laughed in disbelief at all of it.

"It's your son's birthday soon?"

"Yes."

"He is saying 'Happy Birthday' to him."

I had to take a minute then. I couldn't stop the tears from streaming down my face. I was astounded. I was heartbroken. I was happy. I imagined Yannick next to me. What was actually real in that moment didn't matter. To feel defies all reality and makes everything matter, real or imagined.

"Did you write something for him?"

"Yes, I wrote him a letter."

"He is saying thanks for the letter. That he got it."

My heart fell to the ground.

A few months earlier, I had written Yannick a letter. It was a way for me to release him. My healer had told me that his spirit was still attached to me and that I needed to do a release ritual to free him. And so, with my words, I wrote something that I felt would set him free. It was one of the most beautiful experiences of my life. I knew I had to burn the letter next to a body of water, but I didn't know where to go. It was the middle of winter, and I had no idea where to access a shoreline in the city.

I thought about it for a bit, and then I remembered a place I had seen a friend go to. I looked it up and started to make my way there. I drove in that direction and down a road I had never been down before. I stopped where I felt I should stop and looked to my left across the street. It seemed to be the most beautiful vision I had ever seen. I guess it was how the light hit just right and how this beautiful tree beckoned me. Next to the tree, there was a man. He looked back at me as if to signal that this was the place I was looking for. The spot I ended up going to was a little nook on the river shore. I set the letter on fire and watched it burn. I felt like staying there at the shore forever.

I had felt in my heart that the ritual had worked and that my brother was freed to sail away. But now, I am getting this unbelievable confirmation. In the letter, I had told him about a dream that I had, a dream where he was resurrected. He rose from the grave and gave a speech in a pilot's bomber jacket; it was so bizarre. I assured him that I would do what he wasn't able to and break the generational curses of our family.

I could feel now that he was truly at peace. A feeling that he probably never felt while he was alive.

"He is saying that he is sorry that you don't have nice stories about him."

"Oh, that's not true."

"He is saying that he always loved you and always knew that you were an angel. He says to follow your steps and that he is happy he can now watch you from above. He says, 'Thank you, my sister.'"

We took a moment then for a pause. I confessed to Paul that I cry a lot. He then started talking about my career options and asked me what I did for a living. I told him I was an engineer and asked if I should think about leaving.

He replied: "No, they are saying to stay in your career but to ask for a raise. And that there would be another opportunity for you coming in mining. This company would offer you a lot more money, so you can freelance in writing on the side. You do translation?"

"No, I have never translated, but I write. I feel like I channel messages that are healing for people."

"You've been a translator before, for the King James Bible, and you were also a scribe in a past life, an Egyptian scribe. You would translate the sacred texts into the common language. As you expand your consciousness, more of your past lives come through. Keeping a high frequency is key for you, as well as is the practice of automatic writing. This is how your guides will speak through you. When you write, your words come from a 7D/8D frequency. And the way you string words together is healing for the reader. Your mission on Earth is to deliver these messages. You are an old soul. This is your 773rd life on Earth."

The profundity of me made it so I couldn't speak; I was speechless. It reminded me of the first time I saw my birth chart. I couldn't believe that this person was me.

"Do you have any questions for me?"

"Yes, I have one, but I need to tell a story first . . . ."

I started writing soon after I moved to Montréal, to blog about this new life experience. At some point, my writing became therapeutic, and as a result, deeper and more vulnerable, and so I started to take it more seriously. And then, I met an author one day, an author who had written a New York Times Best Seller. We were talking about her doing the research for her next book, and I told her about my passion for writing.

She asked me if I was going to write a book.

I told her that I didn't know. I really hadn't thought about it. I honestly didn't even feel like I was good enough to do that, and then, I had no clue what I would even write about.

Then, something took me by surprise one day. This Instagram account called "Shaman Portal" followed me. I could see they were hosting a shamanic retreat soon. I followed them back, and I felt like this was something I was interested in, but that it wasn't the right time for me to go. I had been quite fascinated by shamanism for a while, so this opportunity seemed divine in its arrival.

Even so, I felt that because of what was happening in my life, I could not go on this adventure yet. But this account kept poking me, and bugging me, and I felt as if it was choosing me. Telling me that I was chosen.

It's strange, but I truly felt like I was one of the chosen ones.

And so I asked the Universe for a sign. And I got one.

I went on my Instagram, and I immediately saw a post from Shaman Portal, advertising a half-price ticket. One major reason I had been hesitant was the price. If I recall, the cost was around

$12,000, which was a good reason not to go. But when I saw that they were accepting applications for a half-price ticket, I felt that this was my sign. And so, I wrote them an email, expressing my interest, and they replied:

> Please let us know of your experience with shamanism, and why you feel the calling to attend this shamanic pilgrimage. We will be considering all applications within the next week or so.

When I thought about my response, I felt as though I needed to stand out from all others, so I felt I should tell them that I was going to write a book about my experience at the retreat. I can't for the life of me understand why I would do this, but perhaps this was the moment I had been waiting for. My intentions were not entirely pure, because I just wanted to save money, but I felt that by writing these words, I was writing my destiny and sealing my fate:

> I have no experience in shamanism. I have been interested though for the past ten years, and have been reading about Carlos Castaneda's journey with Don Juan Matus, so this adventure would be my introduction to it. I have been on a spiritual awakening journey for a few years that has shifted into high gear in the last six months, and to be honest, I just feel like I am being divinely guided towards this retreat.
>
> I am a writer, and that is my way of healing myself and others, and my way of channeling divine messages. So I wanted to use

this experience as a creative opportunity as well, and write about
my experience, and publish the story of my journey in the Andes.

In the end, they awarded the half-price ticket to someone more deserving, I assume. But they decided that because of my heartfelt email they would award me a $1,200 stipend "to make it a reality for you to join the shamans in Ecuador." If I accepted this offer, they asked for me to keep it confidential.

I explained all of this to Paul, adding that I had just received the news of their gift that morning. But despite the signs that the universe had already given me, I still wasn't sure if I should go, so I asked him for guidance.

"Yes," he said. "You're going to write a book about your experience with them. It will tell the tale of a 'New Shamanism.' It will be about the ancient teachings coming back to life. You are of a higher consciousness than them, and so your book will create a bridge between these older traditions and the new form of thought that we represent. We are experiencing the human shift. The book will be called *The History of the Ancient Times* . . . no, *The Future of the History* . . . no . . . it will be called . . . *The History of the Future.*"

PART ONE

ECUADOR

This is how the world was created: Pachamama. We are the micro-organisms of her and all the elements within her, and that's why we must learn to respect her. True knowledge is accumulated in the body, not in the mind, not in the ideas, and that's why we respect our bodies. Pachamama is within us.

—Don Acho

Chapter One

The Harmony Is in Your Heart

Neither Bruno nor I were looking for love when we found it. Love came knocking, and we kept it cool in spite of what we felt on the inside—this feeling that something was growing that could not be contained.

It was a literal door that Bruno knocked on, the door of our mutual friend we had both come to visit at the same time. My friend had gone to the store and never mentioned a visitor would be arriving, so I was surprised to hear a knock. But as soon as I opened that door and saw Bruno, I realized he was the reason I had been carried across the world.

Bruno is one of the most truly unique people I have ever met. He grew up in the Communist era of Romania, and I think it was the thing that shaped him the most. It was the basis of his trauma and fears, but it simultaneously fed his desire to expand and grow. He spent a lot of his childhood with his grandparents. His dad wasn't around, and his mom was in university studying law, so I know he felt a level of abandonment that was perhaps what drew us together:

our trauma bond. I was the not-so-typical, typical black girl from the City of Angels. My father had abandoned us when we were young, and my mother hated him for it. I could never have understood what this felt like, but her hate had created a distance between her and us, so there was this feeling of loneliness that pervaded my youth. At the same time though, I always felt the presence of a higher power, comforting me. I don't know if Bruno felt the same way about God, but I do know he felt the loneliness and the feeling that he could make it on his own, not needing anyone else. And yet, when we started on our journey, we knew we needed each other, and that we couldn't get enough. We engorged ourselves in our love from the start.

We eloped in Paris, creating one of the most beautiful moments I was ever a part of. Walking towards Bruno on a January day and catching the look on his face upon seeing me as his bride was unbelievable. On that day, I told him our love was stronger than death, because it was. But when we took that leap together, we didn't realize that love on its own wouldn't be enough. I'm quite sure we didn't think that far ahead.

We were living by the moment, fully present, which seems like a good thing even though it wasn't. The night before we wed, we had one of the craziest fights of our relationship. We made up that night, and by the next day, it was as though it had never happened. We were wed and said our vows and meant every word.

Then, every now and again, we would get into another fight over nothing. A fight that would tear us apart. It was like a wall would be dropped in between us, a wall that was immovable because neither one of us was willing to move it by admitting we were wrong, especially me. I was about as insensitive as he was sensitive—complete opposites in the worst of ways. But somehow, some form of magic would bring us back together as if nothing ever happened. As if it was simply a door between us again, a door that only required one of us to knock on it and the other to open it with great excitement, leading us back to our happy place. Over time though, this process of finding our way back home got harder and harder. The things left unsaid, and the things we didn't do or address in the right way, started to creep up on us. We were adults who were emotionally infantile, stunted by never being asked how we were feeling or told how important it is to ask.

Shortly after our wedding, I moved to Montréal to start our new life. It was a life that I imagined would be all rainbows and butterflies, the power of love still so effervescent. I had the dream life after all, one where I didn't need to work, one where I could be a housewife, a dream that all of us women are still programmed to dream. It was a dream though, which I would wake up from every day in a nightmare of confusion. I couldn't understand how I could have everything "I ever wanted" and still feel depressed, a feeling I had never felt before. Bruno tried his best to help me, understanding full well the culture shock I was undergoing, but I just wasn't ready to listen. I had to go through this identity crisis on my own. The housewife life just wasn't for me, and I had to find my way back, on my own, through the dark.

We were learning, albeit slowly, that marriage wasn't always going to be a happy time, that it would be filled with many struggles and countless tests, and that we each had a shadow, and that our shadows didn't get along at all. There was always a light though, always a way for us to persevere through the crazy fights we would have where

Bruno would literally throw the trash on the floor and break all the dishes, and where I would give him the most brutal silent treatment. It was certainly the exact opposite of what he truly needed in those moments. It took me some time to understand that all he needed was for me to hold him in my arms.

I think we felt that we would change at some point, by parenting our own inner children instead of parenting each other's. This is when I started to write.

I also started to work again, and Bruno started to build his own law practice. This arrangement worked for us to some extent, but then we would fight again, and go through the same cycle of making up, having a talk about what we would change, and have sex to seal the deal. Our biggest failure came from believing that we could solve the unsolvable, when our darkness kept outsmarting us every time. Our darkness couldn't extinguish our love, but it brought a lot of doubt into how long we felt we could endure this marriage.

At some point, the Divine stepped in to guide us into a more therapeutic way of life. We were guided to a Home, to the most beautiful sacred space in the woods that reconnected us with Nature, with our connected nature. As soon as we stepped through the door, we knew it was ours, and we knew it was a gift. We moved in during the summer, but it was the winter that made us fall in love with it. Perhaps the beauty of a winter in the woods could allow us to endure and to embrace its cold and dark days.

Perhaps.

We had high hopes, and its sacredness fulfilled that, with the millions of stars above, and the fireflies during the summer nights.

Our home brought us so much, but we still seemed to embrace it in different ways because we were just different people. I went towards a more spiritual way of life, embracing all the medicine the Earth was giving me, but I think for Bruno, a house just meant more responsibility, and was something else that he didn't really want. I know he enjoyed our nights sitting by the fire, but perhaps the work of making the fire wasn't something he cherished, whereas I grew to be enthralled by the art of fire making and watching the snow fall so magically. It sparkles, you know.

There was certainly much that we had in common, but it was hard to know what was real and what was simply a compromise. The extent of how much we sacrificed our authenticity to maintain agreeable remains to be known. No matter the mystery of us though, there was no mystery to how the Divine always gave us the lessons we needed. And for us, the ultimate lesson was the ultimate gift: Hugo.

We didn't even try, and there he was in my belly, a light growing within the darkness inside. The name *Hugo* came to us unexpectedly one day. And once I saw that it meant "bright in mind and spirit," I knew it was his name. Hugo was from our hearts. He brought us together in a way we could never understand until we could look back. In the end, it would be Hugo who would heal us with his light.

Hugo was born in the summer, and our lives were blissful and magical for a while. But by the next summer, my brother was dead. And it was like something else was born in that moment.

Just like love, I didn't know what death was, so I didn't know what it would do to me. And just like love, its effects were slow moving and potent in both its wound and its medicine. Death allowed me to see what my purpose is, and with that, the knowledge that Bruno and I had already fulfilled our purpose together.

Bruno is the best man I have known. The smartest; the most talented artist; the most driven, ambitious, dedicated, disciplined person I have encountered. I am different . . . and similar in different ways, and we explored a lot of those commonalities. So, to say we grew apart is inaccurate, as well as boring; we just grew differently. And unfortunately, our growth hadn't yet taken away our pain. Instead of seeing the look of love in his eyes, I started to see the look of pain, and I couldn't bear it. We had been sleeping in separate bedrooms; at first, it was because of the amount of space that Hugo and I took breastfeeding and co-sleeping, but then sleeping apart just became the norm. Bruno and I were living apart while living together. There were so many times that I just wanted to lie with him and hold him. To hold him like the little boy that he still is, sleeping with his grandparents but wishing for his parents. And I just wanted to be held too, like that little girl who slept with her blankets over her head because she was afraid of the dark. There was so much Bruno and I wanted to give, but we were just unable to give it. The darkness was breaking our spirit.

Then, something happened that I would have never seen coming in a million years because I quite possibly traveled a million lifetimes to experience it. I encountered an angel.

He must've been an angel because everything about him made me feel as though anything is possible. That somehow what we had together would change us and maybe change the world. It was supernatural.

To say I was in love would be an understatement.

The gratitude and joy consumed me. I never dreamed that unconditional love could exist between a man and a woman so soon, so mind-blowingly soon, but this was the feeling I felt. I asked the angel his name, and he told me it was Emilio.

We spent a magical evening talking and dancing together, which culminated in a first kiss. I felt like I was in a dream, surrounded by the feeling of a deep connection to Spirit, but something didn't feel right. Something in my heart worried that this was too good to be true.

We started to make our way upstairs to leave together, but before we made it outside, I had an out-of-body experience. Everything slowed down, and something inside of me told me I couldn't leave with him. I knew that I couldn't be intimate with him, but I didn't know how to say it. And I knew that he wouldn't just let me leave, so I just left without saying goodbye. He turned his head, and I was gone. I never imagined doing such a thing to someone I loved so much.

By the next day, I knew I could never go back to who I was. I had felt too much. I had felt what it should feel like to be with the one you love. A feeling that Bruno and I had lost after repeatedly bringing out the worst versions of ourselves. Meeting Emilio woke me up to the fact that there could exist a love greater than what I had experienced. A higher love.

It was the most humbling experience to be understood and accepted in my totality. This experience shook me to the core and broke the shackles holding me back. But it wasn't Emilio who made me feel this way. It wasn't his dreamy eyes and sun-kissed skin, and it wasn't the possibility of running away with him. I realized that what set me free was the profundity of a connection like this existing. What set me free was something that changed inside of me. It was as if through recognizing him, at the soul level, I had recognized myself and who I was meant to become.

It had been almost a year since that night, and I had seen him only once more. I had seen him twice in a year, but it felt as if he was following me everywhere. At home, I felt his presence the strongest, but he came with me to Ecuador as a stowaway.

Emilio was the first of my many spiritual teachers, and he didn't even know it. Now, as I journeyed onward to Ecuador to embrace the wisdom of its shamans, I realized that the story I was living and that I would write was a story of love.

The grounds of Hacienda Chorlavi in Ibarra, Ecuador, felt like a place on Jacob's Ladder. A place where angels traversed on their way to and from heaven. The grass felt greener, and the sun felt brighter as I lay on my back, grasping the blades of grass with my hands. I was waiting for the next master class to start, but I couldn't stop thinking of Emilio for some reason. On most days, I was adamant about letting him go despite his ghostly presence, but today was no ordinary day. Today was his birthday. I had realized it earlier when I was reading the itinerary for the day: June 19, 2019. I had never forgotten his birth date. What a strange coincidence for his birthday to coincide with what is surely to be one of the most important days of my life.

Luckily, I had much to do that day, so I decided to put Emilio out of my head for good, for now. The master class of Don Shairy was starting soon. I got up out of the grass, and out of my fantasy world, and started to make my way to the circular room where the master classes took place.

The first thing I noticed when I entered the room was the picture of Don Shairy on the wall. There were pictures of all the shamans there, but his was of his profile. As I stared at it, I was reminded of Red Cloud, a Native American Lakota chief. I have a book that contains every portrait of Red Cloud made throughout his life. In it he says, "My sun is set. My day is done. Darkness is stealing over me. Before I lie down to rise no more, I will speak to my people." It is the beginning of his farewell speech to the Lakota people, given as he lay on his deathbed. They are words that I can never forget. His spirit reminded me of Don Shairy.

As I stared even deeper into the image of Don Shairy, I felt a powerful presence enter the room. It was him, in the flesh. He had long black hair, slicked back, and was wearing a red sarape.[1] As everyone rushed to their seats, I noticed he wasn't wearing any shoes. He made no introductions before he spoke:

"It's very important that you understand that there is a difference between the dialogue we are having now and the dialogue we have with one another normally. This is a sacred dialogue. And now we will begin to prepare ourselves to have this sacred dialogue. With this dialogue, you will begin to see what it is you wish to get out of this dialogue and this journey. Perhaps you want to heal yourself, or

---

[1] A brightly colored blanket-like shawl often worn by men in Mexico.

perhaps a family member, perhaps your husband or your children. Perhaps you want to change your life because the purpose of it, as you've been living so far, has already been fulfilled. I was once a lawyer with a doctorate; I would never have imagined that I would have been walking on this path. It's true that my parents were shamans. But I was a young student, a university student. And I thought that was a different status, a better status for my life. And I thought that by studying, this would allow me to fulfill my real plan. I was very satisfied to hear people call me 'Doctor.' I was happy. But suddenly there came a great change for me. And with every great change, there is crisis; there is no avoiding it. And for me, the greatest gift I ever had was to suffer for four years and to be in the darkness."

He paused so we could take it in. It was almost unexpected what he said. The thing that is unavoidable is unavoidable for a reason. Life provides us with everything.

"I was suffering by myself, without a wife, a girlfriend, or children. And so I felt completely alone. So I asked the Universe a question, as if I was speaking to any person: I spoke in my own language and I said, 'What do you ask of me? What am I supposed to do with my life? Why have I been a person chosen to suffer? Everyone around me is happy, with children; and I have nothing. Why, God?' I was in such a bad state. 'Forgive me, but I can't anymore. No more suffering.'

"And then a great sign appeared to me: I saw a very big condor one night; at the mountain that's in front of my house, on the night of the full moon. And with a great formation of clouds, there was certainly a condor. And the condor was looking at me, and it was midnight. And so I said, 'Not only can I not sleep, but I am going crazy and seeing things that are not there.' So I doubted what I saw. But this was the first time I could hear what was happening in my heart. And my heart said, 'No, this is for you!' And so I stayed observing, until the clouds disappeared.

"Because I was an intellectual, questions started to come: 'What does this mean? Is it true what I saw? Why was it there? Does it even exist, a white condor?' Because it was a white condor that I saw. 'And what does a condor even mean? What does it mean for me?' And instead of solving my problems, it made them worse. Because now I was doubting myself, and I was even believing I was going crazy. And so signs began to appear, and they said to me: 'You are a shaman.' And I would say, 'This cannot happen to my life! I studied. I am a professional. I just can't be a shaman!'

"And my life got a little worse. For every denial, it became darker and darker. And I kept searching for ways to get out of this dark tunnel, to avoid being a shaman. But it wasn't possible. Every time the situation got worse. If I were to tell you that I had my last shirt on my back and that I was eating fruit straight from the trees, near the mountains—in that situation, one night, I looked at the sky: 'Sacred Universe, I accept my path. I don't know what this journey is exactly, but I accept it anyhow. I ask you to show me the way.' Fifteen days later, my life magically changed.

"My biggest fear at the time was my financial situation. I thought if I accepted this route, I would have no chance for stability. But everything turned out okay. I will always say, this cycle of my life, that this was the best part of my life. That this was the best my life has ever offered me. Without a doubt, I can say this to you: I don't worry about money or accounts. I have what is necessary to live well and to be happy. I have no more worries of debts or issues with bank accounts. I live in fullness. I tell you my story now with certainty. I tell you this story now with certainty because I know you have had encounters with teachers and have heard our testimonies. And so I wanted to share with you this certainty of my life story. This desire to transmit to you that same certainty. That you are here to live the change. That you are here to finally be happy. To have the certainty that you can live well and have the money to support your family and live happily. To say I can heal my family, that I can transform the lives of my family. That should be the mission for your life. And so each of us here now can discover our own purpose, for our life, and that purpose allows us to have strength, to have power, to live and to be happy. This is my testimony to you."

Don Shairy paused then, and as I recall, this was the moment I knew I had to get a reading from him. There was a distinct connection I felt with him. Something I hadn't felt with the other shamans. And he was the only shaman who gave readings. I wondered what type of reading his would be. I knew it would be something I hadn't even heard of. I wondered what about my life he would read. My future? No matter what, I knew that whatever happened and whatever he told me would change everything.

He picked up the large conch shell that lay near his feet, on his altar, and blew into it. The sound reverberated throughout the room. Once it was silent again, he began to speak:

"The great mystery of the flight of the condor is that the condor can fly up to ten thousand meters in the sky. It is the animal that can stay in the air the longest. The condor has the same lifespan as the human; they can live up to eighty-four years old. The first teaching is the Accomplishment of Time. Once the condor has feathers, it has to fly. But the condor is afraid, just like all of us. But the time comes when everyone has to fly. The small condor does not know it has to fly or that the time has come. Its parents come to their nest and take it by the neck to the edge of the nest, and they let it go. The small condor then has to open its wings, and it has to start to fly, and it has to learn. Because if not, it will die. And so the condor gets embedded in its mind that it is a flying entity. If it does not make that first effort to fly, it does not fly. That is the first teaching: the great first attempt that has to be synchronized with the right time. For this to happen, it has to be the right time. For the condor, it's very important to know when it is the time. Because they live very far up where the winds are much stronger, where it is very difficult to manipulate the air and the winds, so they have to know exactly when it is the right time to fly. That is the first teaching. We are synchronized with the cosmic time. The first lesson is finding the right time. We have problems because we have lost that synchronicity.

"The second teaching is Persistence. Once the small condor has attempted to fly for the first time, its parents fly down and pick it up, and take it back to the top of the nest, and then let it go again. In that second attempt, the condor can start to balance itself in the air. In that moment, its parents start to dance for their child. It's a beautiful dance. The teaching is that all knowledge is possible with persistence. We have to repeat the ceremony; we must repeat the ritual.

"The third teaching is learning how to balance. In Indian mythology, the condor flies to the heavens to speak to God every single day and comes back down to Earth with the messages from God. And they say that God is resplendent Light. And they say that this also happened with the hummingbird. The story is that the hummingbird was not happy that the condor was the only one who could fly to the heavens. So the hummingbird placed itself underneath the wing of the condor one day. The condor didn't realize it was there and stretched its wings and flew to the heavens. And when the condor was speaking to God, the hummingbird flew out right in front of God. The resplendence of the light of God was the gift to the hummingbird so that its feathers would be bright. From that time on, the hummingbird's feathers would always have that shine of God."

The translator interrupted him and said that he had only five minutes left. He laughed and said, "I don't know if that will be possible. Okay, one last teaching for today. The fourth teaching.

"When the condor eats, he eats with other animals. And the condor has his food, and the other animals have their food. What's interesting is that the condor only eats their own food, and nothing more. The teaching is that we all have our own opportunities; we all have our own reserves. The problem with the modern world is competition. We want to seize the best opportunity, and in this way, we don't connect with our own opportunity. Don't doubt that each of you has your own choices for how to live. We don't need to look at someone else. We have to connect with our own options, and that is the great mystery of happiness. Don't ever doubt this possibility. There is a time now of great crisis on the planet, but we are all here, and so Pachamama[2] has a chance. It doesn't matter how many we are; we can make that difference. We are all the other wing of this reality, to balance this flight of Pachamama."

For a moment I got lost in Don Shairy's story of liberation. I got so lost that I forgot about the profundity of what I had set out to do in Ecuador. Once he said those last words, the reality came rushing back in. I had a purpose in being here, and I too would suffer in the ways I needed to suffer.

Don Shairy had an adobe dome house in his backyard. It was the first thing I saw when I walked through his front gate. It was on the right, hiding among the trees, but not so hidden. He lived a few miles from the hacienda, on a steep hill, and had the really nice house at the end of the road. It was overcast and chilly, and the mood was a bit weary. I was wearing the same thing I'd worn the entire time: a long black cape and a big black hat. There were four of us who came that day, and we were asked to walk through the house and wait for him in the courtyard. He was the only shaman who gave readings, and we had no idea the kind of reading it'd be.

After we waited for a few minutes, Don Shairy came out of a blue door on the second floor and walked down the stairs slowly. We were sitting on the bench below, watching him walk down. The whole experience started to feel like a dream as soon as he reached the ground of the courtyard and started to speak.

[2]The Cosmic Mother.

"As you walk in the Andes, you will find stones like this that are together. And those you cannot take. Those are to ask the mountain about any situation you are in. You take them on a walk and then you place them as a request. You will walk until you get to the place you are meant to go. You infuse the stone with anything you want to shed, and then breathe into it and ask the mountain to honor your request. Some say it is the breath of life, but it means more than that. I am conveying all my information into this. You have to be very clear. In this way, you register all the information into the stone. You do that so that Mother Earth can take it to wherever it needs to go. I tell you this so you can do this ceremony, this tradition in my garden."

It's hard to describe the feeling I felt when Don Shairy spoke to us in his courtyard. Out of all the spaces and all the moments, this one felt like the most profound. I knew that what he would say to me in the adobe dome would change my life forever. He told us many things that day, and he gave us a special seed from Brazil to take home. He then used the two sides of the seed as a metaphor to describe the dual nature of reality as something that is not a polarity but of a nature that is instead complementary. This filled me up for some reason, and I took this energy with me as I walked into the gardens to find a stone to perform the ceremony. My heart told me where to go, and so I went. I picked up a stone and whispered my wishes into it: "I want more than just the experience of sacred union within me, and between me and my divine counterpart. I humbly request for the opportunity to share my story with the world."

There were so many trees intertwined in the garden, it looked like a jungle. From the angle where I was standing, I could barely see the adobe dome. I had to follow Don Shairy as he led me there. It almost looked bigger at a distance, because once we got closer, it was so small that we had to bend down to enter. I took off my shoes and bent down my head, and I sat down to the right of Don Shairy. He was wearing a white shirt and a thick red belt for protection. He had a small piece of wood in his hand, and he lit it on fire. Then he said, "Tune into your intention for being here." It was silent for some time. "Say your full name four times."

I did as he instructed.

"Through the vibration of your voice, I am connecting to your energy. Please stand up. There is a key phrase for you: a new opportunity. Does it resonate? Does it have anything to do with you?"

"Yes, it could mean a couple different things."

"Feel into it. Because that is the key for this consultation." He continued to stare into the flame for a few minutes. "Turn around." I could hear him making a blowing sound behind me. He blew three times. "Sit down. Repeat your name for me again, please."

"Cherizar." I spelled it for him.

"Did you feel into what it means for you to have a new opportunity."

"Yes."

"What does it mean for you?"

"It is something that has been rising up. It is me stepping into my shoes as an artist, as a writer. I was told that I would write a book about my experience here. To bridge the gap between the older shamanic traditions and the new shamanism of my generation, and of the future generations."

"That's the correct answer. The fire responded, so it is the correct answer. It could be the point of a thread, a very, very long thread that will create a ball. Sometimes only one opportunity opens up, and one must embrace it. Remember my teachings on the flight of the condor. The second teaching is about Persistence. When you persist, your intentions become engraved in your unconscious. So in this way you begin to bring to you the circumstances and the opportunities in a very synchronistic way. And in this way, things begin to coalesce around your purpose. Don't think with your mind or what's going to happen after the book. Or if the book will sell or make enough money. Trust that the synchronicity of your desire and your doing will bring everything to you that you need.

"Remember the guy who created Facebook?"

"You mean Mark Zuckerberg? It's funny that you mention that. For the past year, my Facebook bio has been only one word: *synchronicity*."

"Synchronicity?" he laughs. "The first key is you have a new opportunity. The second key is synchronicity. So you need to trust your power to achieve synchronicity.

"Is there any other situation?" Don Shairy asked.

"Well, there is something that I experienced before coming here, something that I feel coincides with the rise of the Divine Feminine. We called it the 'Goddess Ceremony' experience. It was a ceremony and a dance of our light and shadow. And it was all captured on photo and video. The art is breathtaking. I feel it should be shown far and wide for its symbology and brilliance."

"Wow. Those are kind of like utopic situations. But one must believe in Utopia."

"I do."

"If you don't believe in Utopia, then you will never take a step. And this moment is the time for Utopias. I am on the edge of initiating a new Utopia. I wrote a pedagogy. And they will begin to create alternative schools."

"Wow."

"Yeah." And we laughed.

I would say we both thought of synchronicity again in that moment. I sure did.

"One has to believe in the Utopia. I never believed anything would come of it. And then I got a call one day from a friend who was fed up with his son's school, and his response was how he had just written this book about a new educational pedagogy. This is an example of synchronicity. So now your situation . . ."

The translator yelped as the fire burned Don Shairy's shirt.

I thought to myself and said, "What does that mean?" and we laughed.

"I am going to activate synchronicity. So the book and the key person for your book."

He started then with what he called *Takysamy*. It was his unique system of sound healing, using sacred voice and instruments. After he played a couple melodies, he began to speak:

"Persistence is the key. You need to know that this will not be easy. It's going to take awhile, but you have to really believe that what you are doing is important. If you persist in your mind, you will fail. You need to persist in your heart. Do you understand?"

"*Si.*"

"That's the work you have to do. You have to work more with your heart, because right now you are still very activated in your head. Work more with your heart, and that's the secret.

"Open your arms like the condor. Close your eyes."

I heard four chimes.

"Did you hear the harmony in this sound?"

"Yes."

"That is in your heart. This is the harmony that's in your heart. So you must trust that." He played my heart harmony again. "Turn around." He played it again, and I heard the sound of a bird flying by.

"Your umbilical chakra is really good, and that's really important. That's why we are always protected. Those are the connections we have with the Universe and other people. I felt that yours is good.

"Last message: The Harmony is in your heart."

"*Muchas gracias*, Don Shairy." We both got up and gave each other a big hug. I held on tightly.

I left and I didn't look back, but I left with the knowing that we bonded through Utopia, a vision that could define our entire generation. I may write the story, but we will all hold the light and be the change.

Words could never capture the significant and daunting nature of my encounter with Don Shairy. But as I watched the world pass me by as we made our way back to the hacienda, it was his last words that burned me to my core. Everything I was experiencing, feeling, and reflecting upon led me back to the love swirling around in my heart. It was love that brought me to Montréal, where I created an entirely new destiny as a mother and as a writer. It was love's shadows that led me to understanding the dynamics of a relationship. And then, a supernatural love jolted me into this moment when I could see the power of unconditional love being born again.

The dawn is coming.

Chapter Two

The Children of the Sun

"True wisdom is when you practice knowledge and when you practice it every day. A doctor that has no health is a bad doctor and does not know medicine. So if you want to be healers, you must have a lot of health, and you must show that you are strong. And you must show that the knowledge you have is not only being applied to yourself, but to others."

Don Acho paused and played a little melody on his zampoña.[3] It made a piercing whistle-like sound. He then yelled out "Ahooooooooooo!"[4]

Silence followed. The suspense of what he would say next bound us.

"In ancient times our people would say, 'We are the children of the sun!' In Peru, Bolivia, Ecuador, and all indigenous nations of South America; as one nation, we would yell: 'We are the children of the sun!' Why? Because at one time we lived in the center of the sun. And it occurred to us to reveal ourselves. And so they sent us

---

[3]A traditional Andean panpipe.

[4]*Aho,* which is often likened to the Christian *amen,* is spoken to align with one's higher self and the divine.

to all the worlds, to dark worlds. But our essences stayed, and our desire to return and live in the sun stayed too. We have come to illuminate the darkness."

And it was like as soon as he said it, it was. The darkness began to fall. And it looked like it had traveled through the door and wrapped itself around Don Acho. The darkness embraced him.

Don Acho stood in the center of the circular room where all the master classes took place. He was wearing a dark blue jumpsuit. His hair was jet black, tied in a ponytail. His face was both hard and soft. He reminded me of the mountains and of the moment I saw them for the first time. The darkness had embraced the Andes too, and it was as if the shadow that cloaked them made the stars' reflections shine brighter. I never knew I could see the stars like that. I never knew I could get to know a mountain through the feelings it stirred inside me. I never knew I could get to know a mountain as I moved past and through it. Don Acho was the mountain in this moment, and the mountains were him. He put his hands in front of him, with his palms out, and said:

"The hands are what get energy, and they are also what give it. When we put out both hands, we are activating both the feminine energy and the masculine energy. Sit up now with your back straight. In this form, there is communication. The energy centers are going both up and down. This is why we do this exercise; you are creating energy going up and down—flowing. Going in and going out—flowing. And we are activating the feminine strength and masculine strength. One hand down, one hand up, hands open, palms open, eyes closed. Hear me. Hear me sing to you first. Hear my call."

He started to sing so softly, a long "o," like "Oh my love . . . ." I could hear his voice gradually get louder, and I could feel that what was happening was what I suspected. Don Acho was calling out for the Holy Spirit.

It seemed as though he would never stop this chant, until suddenly he quieted to a whisper. He seemed to be looking for something, or someone. "Where are you, Father? Where are you?" he whispered loudly.

He closed his eyes and started to touch his heart and his stomach. "I want to feel you within me. I want to feel you in my heart and in my solar plexus. I want to feel your superior spirit in all my eternal parts."

He started to sing again, and then he started to shout: "Please, Father, do not leave us! I want to feel you; I want to feel you within me. Forgive me for straying away from you; forgive me for not understanding your teachings. I want to feel you. Please don't abandon me! Oh great Father, come to me. Let me hug you! Let me be a part of you. Let me feel you in my heart, in my soul. Father . . . Father . . . Father!"

His final word echoed throughout the room.

"Lift your arms up and put them above your head like a pyramid, just like I am doing." He played a note on his zampoña and continued: "Put that energy into the pyramid." He picked up his rainstick, and it was like I was there, next to a river rushing by.

"Okay, put down your hands. To start, we are just going to keep our hands above our knees."

Everyone adjusted their hands.

"In this lunar day—lunar because there's always light—we have prayed. We have prayed for the presence of the Great Father, and he is here because we have called him, right?"

No doubt about that.

"And just like a prayer, we must strive to feel our true self, our eternal self, in a simple way."

Don Acho paused, and then switched topics rather suddenly. My mind, however, started to drift as soon as I heard the phrase "true self." This is something—or someone—that has always intrigued me. I feel as though I've been chasing her for a while, chasing her in hopes of not just finding her, but defining her. She has so far proved elusive, but at the same time, I know that it is she who has guided me here, to Ecuador. All this time I thought I was the only one chasing, but perhaps things are not quite as they seem. All I know is that I don't know what she is, but I trust like hell that she's there. I am no one special, but this trust—this trust I have in her—is my superpower.

I started to tune back in to the master class. Don Acho was discussing the diagnosis process of the healer.

"There are so many types of healing. And in some, there must be a diagnosis performed. Some healers use a candle. They rub it all over their client, passing it through all the bodies, and then they light the candle. Through the flame, they can sense what's wrong. There is an electromagnetic connection between the client, the candle, and the healer. But you must be sensible. That's one way to diagnose."

He started to speak very fast and then stopped. The translator directed her words to us then, to explain how he was saying that he gets very excited and forgets that she has to translate and that she has to pick it up. Everyone in the room roared out in laughter then. Don Acho was quite the comical character.

He continued then:

"The egg picks up all the vibration of the person, and it diagnoses the nervous system. You can see how the kidneys are, you can see the prostate, and the womb. There are so many forms of diagnosing.

"Have you seen the diagnosis with a cuy? Have you seen this? It's like a guinea pig. The Ecuadorian healers, especially up here in the mountains, they use the cuy. Its called cuy because when you pick him up, that's the sound that he makes. So they rub the cuy all over your body; all over your back, your legs, everything. And then the healer, with his nails, starts to open the skin, and he looks through the skin, and he can see how the nervous system is, how the urinary system is, and then he opens the stomach, and he can see how the intestines are, how the liver is. And then he pulls out the heart, and he has the heart in his hand while it's still beating. And it is this that tells the healer everything. What the healer sees in the cuy is what is wrong with the patient. It's very sad that this is how they do it, but this is the most precise diagnosis. I had the opportunity to see this firsthand: I had a patient who [fell] down the stairs when she was three and broke a bone in her skull. She was in pain her whole life. And so I did some therapies with her, energetic, so that her brain could get stronger, so she could tolerate the pain. Fifteen years passed, and they did a diagnosis on this woman, with the cuy, and her skull was free of any damage. So my therapies worked, but incredibly the healer could still see that she had a pain in her head. The healer could tell that she had had an accident many years prior. Incredibly, it came out in the cuy. So I understood then how powerful this technique was. I feel bad stripping an animal. But by just rubbing this animal on the body, you can cure yourself of many ailments.

"With the ancestral medicines, there are many ways to heal physical problems, mental problems, and whatever part of the body, and/or any organ.

"In reiki, the healer is giving their energy, and sucking the energy out of the ailing person. So when they say they're only channeling, they are lying. The person who heals connects themselves energetically with the person who is sick and absorbs the sickness and the energy of the person. That is why the healer must be strong, and they must have a lot of energy to share. To heal is an exchange of energy. And to not eat all the garbage of the sick one, to not get affected by their sickness, you must put your hands out.

"The healer also uses other elements. They use extracts, aromas, rocks, and other natural elements to suck the negative energy from the person. It is an energy cleansing. This is why we call it *Limpia*.

"You've seen many different types of healers. So try to be observers and to be observant. Because each one of them [has] years of experience and specializes in a different technique. It's not that if you learn a few healing techniques that you are finished. Life is a constant journey; it is constant learning. And what's most important is to know how to get up and to walk in the way of wisdom. The healing technique you must look for is how to live a real life and how to fight to do it.

"This idea that if you behave you go to heaven in reality is just staying. Because heaven up there, down there, to the right or left—what heaven do we go to? When people start to develop consciousness, they start to live in a world where there isn't a need for a heaven. The purpose of healing is to heal yourself, to find that eternal life and that motive for living. To live in harmony with everything and everyone, with the mountains, and all the animals. But especially with oneself."

Don Acho picked up his zampoña and blew into it with a loud breath. An interlude.

"Sacred Father," he said. And he blew into the zampoña again and again. For a moment, it seemed as though he would continue with the dramatic prayer from his opening, but then he said, "I want you to rub your hands together, and I want you to think about whatever it is you want to ask for. Rub your hands and inhale. Breathe in the elements of what you are asking so that what you ask enters your body, your mouth, and your heart. And that's what shall be."

Don Acho's voice was so haunting, I could still hear it the next morning as I lay in the darkness. I had never witnessed such a thing. We thought we would be witnessing a master share a message that could change the world, but what we actually witnessed was so much more. I can't speak for everyone there, but for me, I knew the performance would reverberate in my being for days to come.

Everyone else had done Ayahuasca[5] the night before, so I knew I would be the only one up so early. Don Acho would be leading the sunrise ritual, where he would teach the ancient Andean exercises. These were core to his healing system. So as much as I wanted to sleep, I knew I couldn't. I knew that this would be something very few would ever experience. And it was because I decided not to do Ayahuasca. It was Paul (the medium), who had advised me not to, during that reading. He said, "Because you are a being that is already at a high vibration, you are already connected to Source. You don't need to bring your consciousness to a different expansion. The shamans are working more on an old consciousness level, and you are at a new consciousness level, so that is where the plant medicine would clash with you."

I could hear his words as I jumped out of bed. It was chilly, so for a moment I thought about getting back into the warm bed. Before I could change my mind though, I got dressed quickly and ran out the door.

The courtyard was empty, as expected. In less than an hour it would be filled with the sounds of breakfast, my favorite meal. It would be such a treat after this workout.

Everything was still except the wind. I took a deep breath and started to make my way to the gardens.

I took my time walking through the courtyard and crossing the bridge over the pond, and it was then that I could see him. He was running in place, by himself. It would just be me and him, as I predicted.

---

[5] A tea made from psychoactive plants, traditionally used by South American indigenous peoples in spiritual and healing ceremonies.

As I got closer, I started to get a little anxious. I didn't want to disappoint him. He was a lot older than me, but I knew he would kick my ass. I started to regret all the times I skipped workouts, which were a lot.

Once I arrived, he just kept running; my arrival didn't change much.

"Take off your shoes and start running," Don Acho instructed.

After I bent down and took off my shoes, I started to follow him as we ran in circles around the yard. We ran for a few minutes, and then without any direction, he started his circuit training. He motioned for me to mimic his movements, and so that's what I did. The communication was visual in this silent ritual, but a lot of what he did was familiar: planks, pushups, and core work. I was keeping up with him so far, but it wasn't easy. He didn't take any breaks in between, so all I had was my will to not give up or look weak.

At some point, he started to change it up and integrate movements that reminded me of the martial arts. They were like blocking drills that used the whole body as a form of protection. Don Acho seemed to be leading me through his yang warrior training. I watched him intently but at the same time soaked and synced into the world around me. I could see a bird watching us as we moved like Shaolin monks, poised for defense, but with grace and beauty. The nature of the yin was hidden but somehow more potent.

My thoughts drifted as we danced. As children, my brothers and I were obsessed with Bruce Lee's *Enter the Dragon*. We watched it a million times, it seemed, rewinding our favorite parts over and over again, laughing hysterically at the sounds and faces of the Shaolin Master. An art form that is combative, a monk who is a fighter.

Seeing Don Acho in this way allowed me to see him deeper than I did during his master class.

As the night became day, a bird started to sing the morning song. We both paused for a moment and took a deep breath as we watched the sun make its way into the world. I realized then that healing takes on so many more forms than we could ever imagine. The healing is done through the healer's ability to allow you to see them. I could see Don Acho, and that was the healing taking place.

He cracked my neck as I lay on the ground next to him, and I began to breathe heavily with the relief that the workout was over. He told me to slow down my breathing, as he broke the silence:

"God loves the one who gets up early," he said. "The elements of health are in the oxygen in the air. And they are collected in those first hours of the morning. Unfortunately, people can't get up that early because at night they watch TV and are on their phones. They are seeing who has said hi to them, and they stay up late at night wasting their energy and their time. The one who wastes time is wasting the biggest capital we have: life."

I noticed that a lot of people had gathered. They had missed the workout but came to hear him speak:

"In order to be connected to Source, and to fly, we must have a clean body. We cannot expect our spirit to be clean if our bodies are not. It starts with the body. The energy of the sun is trapped within leaves. So when you eat the raw leaves, you get the solar energy.

"When people put on plastic clothes, they are isolating themselves from Taita Inti.[6]"

---

[6] The Inca Sun God.

A few in the crowd giggled, but he was right. We were smothered in so much unnaturalness, which raised the question of the rewilding of the human species.

Don Acho spoke about knowledge being in the body and how the brain reacts when we move it. I had for some time been fascinated, driven almost, by this idea of "the collective consciousness." This idea of a shared mind and of the absorption of knowledge swirling in the sea around us. I had always imagined it as something solely based on mental capacities, but I was sorely wrong. *The collective consciousness is a bodily phenomenon.* Something discovered when we dance in the dark for no one, dancing for our pain and for our joy. There can be no real separation between the collective mind and the collective body. The only difference is that one of them can be moved, can be touched, can be seen. And so we move it. The healing that took place that day was a remembrance of my most fundamental nature, transmitted through the sacredness of movement. "The art of fighting without fighting," as a great master once said.

Two days later I would dance in the streets of Cayambe with Don Acho for the Inti Raymi festival.[7] He held my hand and spun me around while surrounded by villagers singing and dancing in unison. We danced all the way to the top of the mountain, to the top of the city where all the families gathered—celebrating in costume, in food, and in dance. I have never witnessed such a celebration of the sun,

---

[7]An ancestral Inca festival honoring the Sun God.

and so I wondered if we as a species would ever get back to a place like this. To a place where we honor the sun and all the elements in this way. A place where we are collectively free to imagine ourselves as children of the sun.

Chapter Three

We Must Give Thanks

When I stepped off the train platform and looked at the San Simeon Piccolo, perfectly framed from afar, all of what I knew to be real suddenly ceased to exist. I had arrived in Venice, the City of Canals, a place where water flowed in the spaces normally inhabited by concrete. It was such a strange feeling, and one of such profoundness. I could say it was the sheer beauty of it all, to be immediately confronted with masterpieces of art and architecture, but it wasn't that. It was something so much deeper inside of me that stirred. An unknown that suddenly became known. A life that I used to live swept over me as the waves crashed on the boat. I looked down at the water and saw a reflection I had never seen, a part of me left unseen . . . until now. A peek of my true self emerged. I hadn't ever seen her before. I became stumped, and yet I still embraced this reflection with everything I had. A knowledge began to fill me up like a water tank.

My cup runneth over into the sea.

Once I was able to reflect on that moment, the words poured out of me like never before.

When I look back at this moment when I fell in love with a place, I realize what really happened was that I started to fall in love with myself. And once I began to reflect with words, I finally became a writer. Something about this place and this past life of mine connected me to the writer within. Up until that point, I had been trying to write but never quite felt like my writing was real. But now it was as if my words had been channeled through the sacredness of an experience, through the embodiment of God. What a wonder is this world we live in!

The idea that sacredness can be both objective and subjective has moved me again and again—to the point where I have become enthralled with the idea of a sacred space. These spaces help me to see me. And now, my journey has brought me to a place where there lives a man known for finding the sacredness in everything, for finding God in everything. The Dalai Lama referred to him as "the Jesus of the Andes."

All of us here call him by his name: Don Alberto.

I encountered Don Alberto for the first time when I was walking through the gardens of the hacienda. I was actually walking to his master class when I saw him sitting on the grass, leaning against a tree. He had the most peaceful, joyful energy, sitting there without a care in the world. He reminded me of the Buddhist monks that I used to teach English to, once upon a time. He was bald and had a Buddha smile. He exuded the kind of joy that you rarely see in people—a joy of enlightenment, detachment, and peace. I could tell he lived in a different reality from everyone else. He smiled at me, and I smiled back. As I walked past him, I knew that this path had brought me to a holy place filled with the holiest people. I walked into the building with the circular room, where all the knowledge was shared, and I sat down. I was incredibly eager to hear from the man who was given the title Master Yachak[8] by the Shamanic Council of South America.

Don Alberto walked into the room, and the first thing he did was play us a song. And then he spoke:

"Good afternoon, from my heart to everyone that is here. For me, it is a privilege and a great joy to be here. I remember my first memories; I was with my grandfather on my mother's side. It's a community that is limited from a material perspective, but it was a very beautiful environment. All of my childhood memories with my family are very nice, very happy memories. All of the people in the city were always telling us that we were poor and ignorant and used a lot of ugly words to describe us. But for me, we were very rich and abundant with a lot of knowledge. The more I grew, the more I would go into the city, and I thought that they were poor. I would tell my grandfather: 'Why do they live like that? It's so sad that they are living like this. They have a tiny space to live; they don't have anywhere to run.'

"Another memory that I have is when people came to do healings with my grandfather, I would leave everything I was doing and run as fast as I could to watch. I didn't know what was grabbing my attention, but when people came, I couldn't not be there. I don't remember how old I was, but I was very, very young. I ran so fast that sometimes I fell, but I didn't care. I would get up and go next

_____
[8] The Quechua word for "ancestral healer."

to my grandfather. I was fascinated by all the treatments he had with the different flowers and the essences that he used to clean everyone. And that's how I grew up. He used to teach me everything when we were at the waterfall and the river and the mountain. Every memory I have is like that, and I have very happy memories.

"Right now, as I am telling you this, I am remembering something. I don't know what had happened, but I was at the river with my grandfather. And I don't know if I fell asleep or something, but I remember that suddenly there were a lot of kids, and we were playing in the water, and we didn't drown. *We were playing inside the water, and we didn't drown.* And we started walking up the river until we found a beach where we kept playing. I don't know how long it was, but suddenly I opened my eyes and my grandfather was still there singing to me. I asked my grandfather: 'What happened? Was I dreaming?' and he said, 'No, you simply traveled through the water.'"

As Don Alberto was saying this, it was as if I could see the children submerged in the water, as if I was character in his memory. And everything was suddenly and conclusively perfect. I knew then that perfection did exist; it's just not what we think it is. Perfection is simply to make the shift from a less perfect state to a more perfect one. *Life is but a dream until what's impossible becomes plausible*, and what was once plausible becomes possible, and what was once possible becomes fundamental to reality. In order to approach the state of perfection, there needs to be a series of infinitesimal leaps of perfection, where the overall process is, little by little, perfected. Life is always finding a way to a more perfect union.

My heart felt some kind of a way with Don Alberto in my presence. We had been surrounded by holy men and women at the hacienda, eating breakfast with them and watching them do healings, but the feeling Don Alberto emitted and his effect on the vibrational frequency of the room were unparalleled. I could feel my heart buzzing, and I could map out his distinctive energy pattern. Don Alberto had his own way of describing perfection:

"I was always taught to have a relationship with the trees, the flowers, and the animals. That all of these things were alive. This is how I grew up. So when in school, they were telling me that the stones, that the flowers, didn't have life, I couldn't begin to understand what they were talking about. I knew that they were going to fail me in class if I said what I felt, but I didn't care. I would always say that there was life in everything. That there was life in the natural elements. For me, this was always the reality. And it was shocking for me, when they said you can't talk to plants or the mountain. I couldn't understand why they were saying that. I was very shocked because my grandfather used to always ask permission and asked them to help him in the healings before he would even get a single leaf from the tree; he would ask for permission and tell them what he will use it for. And he would always give thanks and would tell me that you must always give thanks. And he would always say if there is anything that you should do, [it] is to give thanks. So that is one of the things that I would recommend.

"We always give thanks. Everyone is on the same path, and we can contribute to ourselves and society if we can become more coherent. So if you are going to take a flower, you have to ask permission and tell her why you want her and give thanks. Thanks is one of the most essential things. Most people already know these things and can accept this. But we have to take a little step forward by communicating in the same way we communicate with each other. Tell them with love and with your heart the same way you would tell someone you love. Without making any effort, and with a lot of honesty and authenticity."

I mean, could there be a world more perfect than the one Don Alberto paints for you?

"Please tell me if at any point you do not understand something. Just ask me. This is not a classroom, and I am not a teacher. We are sharing with all of our hearts so this can be beneficial to all of us.

"This song that I played at the beginning. I asked for permission from all the elements and all of the directions. And I paid my respects and gave thanks to Pachamama. Pachamama is our Cosmic Mother. Some people get confused and think that Mother Earth is the same as Cosmic Mother, and everyone just says Pachamama; but they are different. Mother Earth in Kichwa is *Alpamama* or *Ashpamama*. The last book I wrote talks about this.

"So one of my recommendations is to make intimate contact with the elements of Nature, without repeating things by memory. You have to feel it. In that moment when you say it, you must really feel it. You must say it with intention and with your heart. We usually do this. Between humans, we do this. Like when you speak to the one you love, do you repeat something you memorized, or do you say something from your heart? Do you agree? It's an invitation. Like when you serenade the moon and the stars, you do it with your heart.

"Whenever we begin to make this intimate contact, all of the elements of Nature are willing, and they want to help you in any way that you communicate. Like at first when someone introduces you, you have some level of a relationship. Afterwards you start laughing, you start chatting, and the level of appropriateness is different. And then you meet again, the level of relationship becomes bigger. Until it comes to a point where you get into an intimate relationship, and then anything you ask of them, they will do it. If you ask a favor, they will do that without a doubt. Do we agree? Is it true? And that's why we get married. And that is how we have to behave with every element of Pachamama. Just like it is between humans; nothing is forced. It has to flow.

"In Kichwa and in all the Andes traditions, we don't have the word *shaman*. In Kichwa, in the native languages, we call the things that I am doing *yachak*. The word *shaman* comes from some writer or interpreter. Someone who wanted to describe characters like us came up with this word. So *shaman* is a general word to refer to wise men and women. Is that true?

"So when you have developed these intimate relationships with the elements of Nature, you can ask for anything that you want. And what do you say to a friend who does a big favor for you? You give thanks. Let's always do this. Give thanks to the sun, to the water, to the rain, to the Earth.

"The yachak path is a path of harmonization with yourself and with everything that is around you. This does not mean that the walker will not have any problems; the problems a lot of times are very necessary. Difficulties teach us more than when everything is good.

"Let's observe the two biggest flying birds in the world: the eagle and the condor. They wait for a big draft of wind that is coming against them, because this guarantees to them that they can fly high. They are not saying, 'I don't like this strong wind.' I am not saying that you should be calling difficulties to your life. But when we are walking, there will be sticks and thorns, and you will walk into a hole at some point. That is part of the path. And let us give thanks.

"We have to give thanks to the things we don't like as well as the things that we like, because it's easy to give thanks to the things that we like. The interesting thing is to give thanks to something you don't like. Who here hasn't had difficult times in their life? But after we pass the difficulty, we have more clarity, more wisdom. Is that true?

"Now I will sing a song, so that we can plant the seed for everything we have talked about. Is that okay?"

I must admit that the idea of talking to plants and animals is not at all weird to me. There is a part of me that already sees the world in this way and a part of me that has yearned to embody it. I feel that deep down we all wish to have this level of intimacy with the Nature that we are. And this coherence Don Alberto spoke of holds so much meaning because it is our incoherence that is killing us. This is heartbreakingly clear. Our incoherence within Self and with each other is due to our incoherence with Nature. The moment our civilization advanced past the agricultural era was the moment we started to lose sight of the importance of what we once had. I believe wholeheartedly that the era we are entering is when we will remember this, and we will start to give life and give thanks to the sacred elements that we are: fire, water, air, and earth.

The more and more I listened to Don Alberto speak, the more I felt these invisible, unconscious things coming to life within me. It's as if my body was remembering the things that it used to know. We are, as a globe, discovering what is deeply buried in our bones: an ancient knowledge being renewed.

After the master class ended, a woman named Susan stopped me on my way out. She is an American too, but I hadn't spoken to her at all. I was surprised to learn that she had been specifically looking forward to getting a hug from me. We had all been getting more intimate slowly, but her enthusiasm was truly flattering. I didn't quite know what to say, so I just gave her the most amazing hug. It felt like presence and like our bodies could in that moment communicate and exchange energy on a level I had never experienced with a stranger. She told me I was beautiful.

I had learned a bit more about how the world sees me. I realized I was somehow meant to give life-changing hugs, and this realization reminded me of something I had once read: you will find out who you are through what someone else tells you. We are all mirrors and have a level of accountability in this work taking place. And it all ties into the coherence that Don Alberto spoke of. Everything connects.

I told Susan that I would meet her for lunch soon, and I continued my way out the door and into the sun.

I hadn't realized it before, but I realized then that the light here was different. Or maybe it was just in that moment, after everything I had absorbed in my heart, I had begun to see everything with new eyes.

I left my encounter with Don Shairy with so much reverberating inside of me, but more so with the knowledge that there was so much more to come. I had a healing with Don Alberto, and I couldn't even fathom what that would be like.

All of the shamans had a sacred space at the hacienda—a place where they could have their altar and lay their head to rest. This was also the place where they performed their healings. Don Alberto was staying in the building next to the playground, and as I approached, I could see him standing outside on his terrace with his apprentice, Isabella. I had actually met her on the first day of the summit before I ever saw him.

She and I, along with all of the women at the retreat, had a very intimate experience. We all sat in a circle and shared the most vulnerable parts of themselves. Isabella shared with us that she had been raped and that this experience led her into a darkness that Don Alberto saved her from. She knew that this was her path. A lot of women shared stories of rape that day; it is frightening to know how many women have been traumatized in this way. The only light is that these experiences had somehow guided them to a place where they gained the strength to share their story.

Isabella also shared with us that Don Alberto had told her that a great prophecy was coming true. That the age of the Divine Feminine had come, and that this energy would bring the world back into balance. As women, we had all felt this energetic shift the most, so for me to hear this revelation was mind-blowing. It felt as though the future of humanity was somehow in all of our hands and that this was why the shamans had heard the call that the time had finally come for them to share their teachings with the world.

I stepped onto the terrace just as the sun began to disappear over the horizon, so I had everything I needed. I greeted them, smiled, and took a deep breath. I could hear my heart beating. I was nervous.

I looked at Don Alberto, and I looked at what he held in his hands: a drum and its companion, a drumstick. He asked me what my intention was for the healing. I thought deeply, and the answer came immediately; it was obvious. Don Shairy had told me my book would be written by my heart, not my mind. So I told Don Alberto that I wanted to be led by my heart, that I wanted my heart to be made strong so that it could lead me to where I'm going. He nodded silently and started to play a song for me. The sound that I needed was the sound that has always existed. The sounds from us and from our oldest instrument.

As he played the song, I thanked him silently for doing it. I gave thanks for many things as he played the drum of my heart. But the thing I gave thanks to most of all was the pain that I had buried there. I gave thanks to the thing I didn't like the most, only to realize that it was that thing I had learned from the most.

Hello, Darkness, my old friend. I just wanted to say thanks and to tell you that you're beautiful. I imagine us walking hand in hand as you hold the stars above the sea. We could be two peas in a pod, you and me.

Darkness had fallen on the hacienda by the time I made it back to my room after my healing with Don Alberto. Darkness fell, and the dark passenger of Death followed me. Grief and the memories it brings still overtake me at times, to remind me of my moody companion. This time it felt different though; my heart spoke this time, and it reminded me that it was Death that had taught me everything I knew about Life.

My heart also reminded me that it was Death that had taught me everything I knew about love too. That without having traveled to the depths of my pain, I would've never known how much love existed down there too. The darkness showed me all the light that I never knew was there. I don't think Death knew what I was able to do with its energy. Because if it did, I'm not sure it would follow me around so much.

Don Alberto played his drum for the last time on February 1, 2022. I can still hear it, and I will forever feel it being played on my heart. I will always remember the light of Don Alberto. He didn't see himself as being any different from anyone, even though he was the most different, the most sacred.

Chapter Four

To Be Born Again

When we were young, my brothers and I used to camp where the buffalo roam on Catalina Island. We would run from one harbor to the next, cutting across the steep hillside at night, and I can still see how the moon lit up the minerals in the sand. I would pretend that they were fireflies even though they didn't exist there. One time we wandered so far from the road that the only way we saw to get back was through a buffalo herd. I remember looking down into the valley and seeing hundreds of them. We were scared, of course, but we were kids, and when you're a kid, you have a way of dealing with fear that is somehow superior to adults. For us, it was the adventure of a lifetime, so we went, led by Yannick. We trudged through the marsh, hiding ourselves in the tall grass, and I don't know how, but we were able to sneak past them unscathed. It all seems like a dream now.

The beauty in the uniqueness of Catalina, and all the unforgettable things we experienced there, makes me realize how special our childhood was, despite all the struggles we faced. Our stepdad, Matt, who was born and raised on Catalina, gave us the gift of being able to live there. So even though our dad wasn't around, we had our mom and Matt, and we had each other. On the surface it seems that this should have been enough, but perhaps this is just a nice story we tell ourselves. It wasn't enough for Yannick, because the healing never took place. Out of us three, he was the only one who remembered when my mom and dad were together. Imagine as a four-year-old seeing your dad one day, and then the next, for your dad to be gone, never to be seen in the same way again. We would see our dad from time to time, but it wasn't enough. More important though is that we were never asked how we felt about it all. *We were never even asked: "How are you?"* Instead, we were all just left in some form of survival mode, in search of a childhood that we could never get back.

Willpower was on my mind as we made our way to the home of Don Oscar. There were about ten of us going, and we were on a big bus. We were making our way up into the hills of Ibarra, on a starry night. Don Oscar spoke to us about willpower during his master class, but he didn't call it that. I've noticed this about many of the shamans. They are so humble about what they do that they don't use egotistical words to describe it like I would. To me it is willpower, but to Oscar, it's tenderness.

Don Oscar took his place center stage with an air of confidence and humility. He was wearing a white collared shirt, a light brown Panama hat, and a thick red belt. He had brought all of his instruments, his offerings, and his son, who was dressed just like him. His energy was very warm and welcoming. I could tell that in everything he did and said, it was important to represent who he was and where he came from. He stood proudly next to his altar, in the circular room, and began to speak:

"Once again, thank you so much for including me in this illustrious gathering. It's a huge honor and privilege to be here. To share the honors that I have. To share the wisdom and guidance that I've received. I'm going to talk about the medicines and the plants, and how they have guided me to do the work that I do.

"On this path of life, many of my teachers have showed me that I am nothing. That it is Mother Earth who informs us and teaches us and shows us what we have to do with our families, and our community. This is why in my family, in my lineage, we do not consider ourselves people with power. We think of ourselves as people who have a tremendous responsibility.

"My mother and father taught me the power is in Mother Earth and all the elements, and that is what does the healing. Once I began to receive the teachings on how to use the elements, I could see how theoretically a certain plant cures, but my head would ask me why: 'Why is it this plant?' So I tried to be guided by my heart, and my heart told me that it isn't one specific plant that works for one person. I realized that every petal, every plant, every stone, is a medicine. So my teaching was to really learn from every tree, every plant, every animal, and every wind that blows on me.

"Through this learning process, I began to speak to them and to connect to them. My ancestors call this 'the language of nature' and how you feel their feelings and to be aware if they are not ready to help in a certain way. So I found that there was a key, a sacred word, which is *respect*, and *gratitude*. So it was like receiving the key to a vault that I just had to open, and I would get the answer.

"This is the experience in my family, and for thousands of years, this is how my family has practiced, and this is what I will demonstrate. Following this path and this teaching has been quite difficult. I think that this is the path that all of you are on in this moment, and I want to tell you to not be deterred by these difficulties. It's about having the respect and asking the favor to be given the key to heal. All of us, from the youngest to the eldest, all have the capacity if we connect with and respect Mother Earth.

"It's important to know certain things, and to know certain plants, and to know how to do the work. I brought some plants, some instruments, and some medicines that I made for you this morning. It's very important to not gather and accumulate things that may unknowingly hurt someone. It's important to know that a stone for one person may feel female, but to someone else, it may be male.

"For me, everything is in its natural state. The air is in its natural state: pure, clean. The earth is full of its gratitude and power to give life to everything. And it's not dirty. The same with water, a piece of wood: it's neutral. So, when I take a stone and I personify it for myself and I give it a name, this person, this stone becomes my friend, becomes my family. Same with a plant. I began to communicate with it, with respect and gratitude. Sometimes, I must smell it to hear it, to feel its energy, and then I know its name and if it's a male or female, and what it can help me cure. But I can't say that this is for that. In the community next to me, the same plant that I use for this purpose, they use for another purpose.

"It's like the air, like when there is a lot of people, the air gets heavy, and we think of it as bad air because it's heavy, but air is air. So what I try to do is lighten the weight. So in this moment, in this space, if I feel something heavy, I give gratitude to this space, to this time. A sweet fragrance, some heat, some plants, so the air becomes lighter. This is a language that it is in my way of being, and I have learned to use this in the work that I do.

"Another characteristic that I have found very important in my family is not to see something as either completely pure or completely impure. Everything is in its natural state of being. It is only with our intention, and the way we ask for its help, that it becomes what we need it to become.

"For something that is unknown to me, I ask this thing that is unknown to me: 'How can we become friends?' Sometimes it takes several days and nights for me to be able to come into communication with this unknown being. And once I realize that this unknown being is no longer unknown, there is one new being in my path now to help me out. We call them *ushai*, something that is there but not visible with the eye; something we cannot touch, but we know is there. Only through tenderness with this unknown being can we become filled with gratitude and come to experience the unknown, become the known.

"I was able to demonstrate this with people in the United States. In 2007, I was invited to do a demonstration in Colorado. The person who invited me was an herbalist, and she took me to the mountains to explain to me the plants that were there, with all of her students. She said, 'Be careful. There is a poisonous plant. You can't come close to it.' And everyone agreed. But while everyone was distracted, I stayed back. That what was unknown and mysterious called to me, and so I got closer and asked, 'Who are you? Why are people scared of you? What do you have for me? May I feel you?' I don't know if it was the wind, but it was a yes. And so I took three small leaves, and with all my heart and emotion, I started chewing them. I then asked my friend what would happen. She said the effects would come in three days.

"I waited a few days, and then weeks went by, and nothing happened.

"So things that, for certain people, are poison, for me become medicine when taken in very small amounts. This is what I learned from my grandparents. The medicine that our grandparents gave us wasn't sweet, wasn't nice; it was always bitter, and we were scared to take it. When I became conscious of reality, the bitter medicine wasn't quite as bitter. And this is the way to receive the medicine in this experience."

When we arrived at the home of Don Oscar and I stepped onto the ground, I looked up and felt as if I could touch the stars. They seemed so close, and everything seemed to be so magical. It was cold, but I could feel the warmth of Don Oscar's home. I could feel the warmth of the people who were tending the fire and the warmth from Oscar's smile. He had one of those smiles that just lit you up—a perfect greeting.

Don Oscar said that some of the village children would join us as well, so there would be fifteen people in the *temāzcalli*.[9] He then directed us to get changed and make our way into this large, canvas tent. We all awkwardly changed in front of each other and then entered the tent, one by one, until the tent could fit no more. It was full.

We all sat together inside in the darkness, and then the keeper of the fire placed several volcanic rocks into the middle of the tent. It was time for the temāzcalli to begin. We had no choice but to be ready for the smoke, and for the fire, and for the darkness embracing us.

Don Oscar told us that there are four stages to the ceremony and that it was important for everyone to stay lucid during the journey. So he spoke to us the entire time. He told us stories and he sang us songs, and I couldn't believe that someone could talk that long. It was superhuman. I had my eyes closed for most of the time because of the smoke, and I kept myself as close to the ground as I could. But even so, even if my eyes were opened, it would still be dark. You think it's the heat that gets you, but it's the darkness. The only light is the light of the fire and the light within you. You have to find the light in you to get through. The light in me is my son. So in the temāzcalli, I held on to the light of my sun.

I didn't want to choose a name for him; I didn't want to choose a name for my son. I wanted it to happen naturally. I wanted for me to just hear it and know. And that's how it happened. When I heard his

---

[9] A traditional Mesoamerican sweat lodge.

name for the first time, I knew it was my son. And when I get to see him, even if I just saw him, I can't believe it; I can't believe he's mine, even though I know he's his. I don't know what I ever could have done to have the opportunity to see someone so beautiful. I don't understand people who don't want children.

The day before my son was born, I was so anxious to see him. I got to the point where I started crying and pleading because I just couldn't wait any longer. I started having contractions immediately. Hugo had heard my call. I labored at home for as long as I could, but then I felt it was time to go to the hospital. As soon as we got there, my water broke. Then I found out I had a bacterial infection, and hospital staff were worried about the baby being exposed to it (since he was no longer protected by the amniotic fluid). So they forced me to get induced, which didn't work at all. Twenty-three hours later, I was still only four centimeters dilated.

Hugo's heart rate started to drop then, every time I had a contraction. Doctors said I would have to get an emergency C-section. I had held out from getting an epidural up to this point, but now I would have to do that and get cut open. I wanted a natural, drug-free labor, but that obviously wasn't working out in the way that I had planned. By this point, I didn't care; I just wanted to see my healthy son for the first time.

And God said, "Let there be light!" And the bright lights of the operating room filled my pupils, and I heard Hugo cry out for the first time. I still couldn't see him though. There was a curtain in between me and everyone. I was anxious. I was so anxious to see him. When would I see him? Then, finally, Bruno brought Hugo next to me, next to the right side of my face. I was frozen so I could barely move, but I managed to look over my shoulder and see his big bright brown eyes for the first time. Wow, I couldn't believe it. Hugo was home. A soul that I've known for lifetimes, reborn again.

Then I had to be taken to the recovery room, so it was only a moment that I saw him. He spent his first hours of life with his father, and that makes me so happy. I, on the other hand, spent the first hour of Hugo's life in the recovery room, shaking uncontrollably. I guess this is what the epidural does to you. It was one of the scariest feelings of my life. It is a feeling I would never wish on anyone. I thought that I would never stop shaking. I truly thought that. And as they wheeled me towards the room where Hugo was, I thought that I wouldn't be able to hold him. But as soon as they put him in my arms, the shaking stopped, and it was as though something within his essence took all the horror of labor away. That it was all just a memory. That it was all just a memory that I would write down one day.

In the end it's more than a memory. In the end it was a place and time I traveled through the psychoactive sweating of my body. Just to be reminded, just to feel again the fact that it will be Hugo who will give me the light to stop the shaking. To stop the shaking within that no one sees, the shake of the childhood trauma I carry for us all. In the darkness I saw the pathway through our children to do something different and to evolve the species through the passing of generational wisdom (true wealth).

Temāzcalli means "to be born again." It is to gestate in the womb of darkness and to re-emerge into the light, cleansed of all sins. And that is how we, all of us inside that canvas tent, emerged a couple hours later. I could see on everyone's faces how we all felt like new people. I wasn't quite sure how I had made it, but I was so proud of myself. There is nothing more beautiful than knowing you've done something great.

I never imagined having the capacity to do any of these things. To live a life so full of life. In the end, we sing songs and play music, we pray and fall in love, and we have children and heal. And in the end, in some way, shape, or form, we make it back to the beginning, to do it all over again.

Chapter Five

Planting Seeds for a New World

By no real fault of their own, our parents convinced us that we needed them. That we needed them to provide for us and to teach us how to be in the world. But upon becoming a parent myself, I realized that what our parents led us to believe was a lie. The truth is that I have never needed anyone more than Hugo, and that it is he who has provided for me in ways I could have never anticipated. If it weren't for him, I wouldn't have been able to get through any of the big transitions in my life. It's crazy to think, but it's true. This is the vulnerability that our parents hid from us to appear strong. They hid from us that they needed us even more than we needed them.

I can distinctly remember the last time I said "I love you" to my mom as a child. I must've been around four, and she had just gotten home. I can still see her walking towards me, towering over me as she responded, "I love you too." We lived in Long Beach back then, in a little house on a cul-de-sac. I don't know what happened after this day, but I never would say those words as a child again. And I would never hear them either. As a result, communicating the needs of my heart is not something I feel safe doing. And even though now I say and hear plenty of "I love yous" from my mom and my family and friends, I still feel blocked. Perhaps this is why I have found myself in this place.

There is still pain in my heart, but not enough to not show Hugo the importance of saying those words. It's ironic that because of what I didn't receive, I know precisely what to give. And yet, it also makes a lot of sense, the paradoxical way of things. So I will fill his cup until it runs over into the sea of self-love. Hugo will know what love is, and he will never doubt that he is my heart.

Hugo turned four a couple weeks before the retreat started. I had traveled without him before, but that was for work and was for the bare minimum of time. I don't know how he felt, but I surely couldn't last very long without him, so I had delayed my arrival to the retreat to be with him and as a result had missed a very important master class: the master class of Doña Susana.

Doña Susana was not the only female shaman there, but she was the one I knew could answer the question "What is the Divine Feminine?" The answer was something I understood in my bones but not quite yet in my head. It was something I felt when I danced, and something I recognized from its radiance and power, but it was something I could not yet describe. I knew that this was the last key to my mission but the first reason I had come. Its rise in the globe could not be ignored. The future had become female overnight, and I knew Doña Susana could tell me why.

I could see her from a distance. She was wearing all white. A white skirt, blouse, and shawl. She wasn't alone, but I didn't care. I was drawn to the fragility of her light. I knew it was her, even though I didn't know her. She was sitting on a table in the courtyard, to the right of the fountain. All the tables on the terrace were beautifully decorated, something I had greatly appreciated during my stay. But there she was, one of the most revered shamans at the retreat, sitting on the most undecorated table of them all.

After watching her for a few moments, I began to make my way towards her until there was no distance. I greeted her and the woman she was with, and they invited me to sit down. The sky was so bright in the courtyard that morning, but I didn't notice until I sat down. Doña Susana and the woman were in the middle of a conversation, so I listened in as she discussed her work with women, where she helps them to recuperate the sacred memory stored in their hearts. She refers to the heart as the first womb. I thought then about asking her directly about the Divine Feminine, but instead I thought I would tell her a story and ask for her advice.

I told her that during the winter, something inside of me told me to walk to the west side of our chalet in the mountains. So I walked between the mountains of snow, and I saw a black bird lying on the ground. One of its wings had been torn off, and the blood made a trail to the body. I felt that I was supposed to find it for some reason, so I instinctively buried it in the snow, laying my friend to rest in the earth, with dignity. When spring came, I remembered my friend, and thought that I should see if she was still there. Sure enough, a black-feathered wing was there, among some other feathers, and I had the instinct to pick them up and to save them for some reason. I told her that I was walking blind but walking straight, as if I could see. And now I was here in Ecuador, two months later, watching the shamans heal and facilitate ceremonies with these feather wands. I could see that for the Incans, the feather was a sacred tool for ritual. I told her that I thought I was supposed to make a feather wand from the bird and that she had died for this reason. Doña Susana immediately agreed and told me how to disinfect the feathers and make the wand. I knew that this ritual was just the first of many that she would teach me.

After our conversation, I walked away in sort of a trance. I felt as if I was in a painting called *Conversation in a Courtyard*. It was impressionistic, but the wings of Susana were undoubtedly clear. Before I left, I told her I would be seeing her again, really soon.

I could hear dogs barking in the distance as I made my way through the courtyard and over the bridge. The sky was overcast, but the forecast was not rainy. Doña Susana was hosting her healing sessions in a small yurt in the gardens. I entered the tent, and to my surprise there were three other women there: Susana's daughter Gabriella and two other women from the retreat. "It would be a Circle," I thought. A *Talking Circle* is the sacred indigenous practice of holding space. It is where we learn how to show up for others and ourselves, by speaking from our heart of hearts, but most importantly, by truly listening. It is not a conversation, but an opportunity. An opportunity to reveal the depths of our darkness.

I looked around the tent, and I could see drums, rattles, and other indigenous instruments; and I knew Susana and Gabriella were singers. I realized then that all the shamans I had connected to most used sound to heal. It's as if through sound we can see and understand everything we are and everything we are not. It's as if through sound we can transpose time and travel into the quantum reality of our interconnectedness to reveal the love at our core. Does sound carry memories too? It must. Because when I look back, I realize music has defined my entire existence. My parents' love for Gino Vannelli gave me a name, and Bruno and I undoubtedly connected through our love for music and its wild ways. I wonder if we, as a globe, can redefine our entire existence with a song. Or perhaps the sound of silence would mark our utopia.

Susana started the Circle by praying, and then she began to tell us her story. She told us that chanting had changed her life. That it had reminded her of who she was, and of the parts of herself that she had lost. And as she spoke, I started to feel a surge of knowing. I knew then that I would lead this sacred practice for the women back home. I knew that the power of the Circle would be a distinctive mark in my earthly mission. When it was my turn to share, I was ready to tell my story.

When I was four years old, my half brother was molesting me. He had a different father, and he was much older than me and my other brothers; he was a teenager at the time. These moments of molestation are some of my earliest memories. He would ask me to come into the room, and I would know what was about to happen, but I was helpless to do or say anything to stop it. I don't know how long this went on, but in the end, my brother Yannick, who was only two years older than me, was the one who saved me. He knew that something wasn't right, and he told my mom.

I have a four-year-old son, and when I think of this experience from all angles, I feel for myself of course, but I feel most of all for my mother. I could never imagine hearing that someone was doing this to my child. Strangely enough, I found my mom's journal once I had gotten older, and I saw the entry she wrote about this part of my life. I couldn't believe she had written about it. Her journal entry made me feel her devastation from the experience, and it strangely comforted me to know how much it had affected her too. I wish she could have talked to me about this, even though I was too young to understand. I just wish she could have talked to me more about everything and asked me how I was doing. The emotional neglect kills me still. I can't blame her, because it was all she knew and all she ever experienced too. But that curse ends here. It ends with me. My brother Yannick wasn't able to save himself, but he was able to save me. And I would like to think that I was saved for the very purpose of ending all these generational curses.

I shared this story, and Gabriella and Susana started to beat the drums slowly, and a crescendo started to build. Gabriella closed her eyes and put her hand on her heart and started to speak to me: "Your son will be a good man and will respect women. He will be a good husband, father, and maybe a good brother."

My Sun. My son. My son who remembers everything. I don't know how, but he remembers everything. Knowing this and knowing what he's been through because of the divorce hurts me more than perhaps any other wound I have. I know he won't remember the time when his dad and I were together, but the guilt I carry for not being able to give him the perfect life he deserves will haunt me for some time. I sighed and started to cry.

At some point after the breakup, I completely checked out, and soon after, Hugo flipped out. I had picked him up from the daycare at the gym that his dad went to, and I didn't let him say goodbye to his dad. It honestly just slipped my mind because I was so focused on myself. For too long I had been focused on only my pain and had not seen his. But in that moment, he told me through what looked like dystonic muscle spasms as he screamed and desperately tried to escape his car seat. It scared me to my core. I have never been as scared as I was then, seeing how much our brokenness had broken him. And from that moment on, everything changed. He held that mirror up to me, and I was horrified by what I saw. So I made a promise to him that day that I would always pay attention. And that I would never let my traumas bleed onto him ever again. That whatever generational curses I was meant to break, I would. So that he would be free.

"You can always sing to that little girl inside of you; sing to her. So we will sing to that little girl, and heal that relationship with your mother and grandmother. We will sing a song to heal these wounds, and it will be a song that you can sing to your son."

Doña Susana began to sing: "Fly like an eagle, fly so high. Circling the Universe, with wings of pure light.

"Fly like a butterfly, fly so low. Circling the Mother Earth, with wings of pure love.

"*Tai witchi tai tai Witchi tai o Ho witchi tai tai Witchi tai o.*"

After we finished singing this song, we all cheered, and then Doña Susana said, "We recommend in order for you to keep this memory of chanting that you always practice relating to the Earth, your own ways of connecting to the Earth. Wherever you are, the Earth is wise. Look to your strength, and your yoni, coming into your heart, and with breath, becoming one. Serving a higher purpose with your mind, with your brain. So that it is real within you. Yes.

"What saved you? As you said before, it was your brother. Because he saw it and caught it. For most of us, no one sees it, but in your case, he saw it. And that's great because he came and said, 'Hey, I'm here.' He is always with you and will always be with you. I can feel your love for him."

Gabriella then asked: "Do you feel that you were repressed or there was a voice that was shut when you were little, or do you feel like your voice is heard and that you can speak your truth all the time?"

I let out a big sigh, with tears welling up. "I don't feel repressed anymore. Writing has been a way of opening up. I know that if I can't speak it, I can write it. In a lot of ways, that was why I was able to leave my husband, because I was able to say it even though it was really hard."

Doña Susana continued, "Today we touched the yoni. And this opens the pathway to your heart, the communication to your heart. So maybe every day you can open this avenue of communication by doing it in the mirror and saying (to your yoni): 'I love you and respect you; I honor you.' And you need to tell this to every woman you encounter because we need to remember that.

"The Circles are a great instrument. These are called the 'messages of the great mother and father.' These are great instruments. Some messages are: 'I love you, I see you, I love you for who you are. I will be here. I will be there for you until the end of time.' You can imagine your mother saying this to you, to your inner child, cultivating a relationship with Nature, yourself, and the world around you. How do you feel about singing?"

I said, "I love singing,"

Doña Susana said, "Do we know a song that she can share with the Circles she will lead? We know an African song that I want you to record for the group."

She then began to sing to me, and to teach me a song named "We Are Marching in the Light of God." There are only four lines that are repeated: "We are marching in the light of God. We are living in the love of God. We are moving in the power of God. We are dancing in the joy of God."

We sang this song a few times together, and then it was time for me to leave the Circle. I would be seeing Doña Susana later for the closing ceremonies, which she would be leading. I gave her a big hug and then left the tent.

As I walked away, I could feel the lesson I had sought sinking deeper and deeper with each step. Perhaps it would sink so deep that I would immediately forget until I needed to remember again. The Divine Feminine was certainly an energy all beings possessed. An energy meant to lead her masculine counterpart, to show him the way. Because the Divine Feminine is a leader. She is also the receptor, the pathway to receiving all the love we so deeply yearn for. So, in essence, she is something that we all will possess in some way, and yet, she is also something that we can't all possess. The yoni is the pathway to a higher embodiment of the Divine Feminine.

I also will never forget how Susana kept saying, "Chanting changed my life." And how, when we were singing together, it felt as if we could shift and bring balance to the world, with just a single note. The feeling and the sounds brought me back to the ancestors I sought, the ancestors I was being guided to seek again. To reconnect with the roots that I felt were cut and the song that I struggle to sing because I don't remember how to let it all out. There was a vulnerability encapsulated in this space that only a group of women could create. We are the givers of life and the ultimate guides for our children.

We are Women.

I could see the clouds closing in on us as I walked through the gardens of the hacienda. It looked like rain, or one of those days where you keep thinking it will. I couldn't stop touching this bracelet Doña Susana had given me. It was a red string tied around my right wrist;

it was for protection. She said that I should wear it for as long as it stays on, and that I would know when it's time to let it go. A few hours before, we had all traveled to a sacred lake fourteen thousand feet in elevation, in a region called Mojanda. It was where the clouds touched the sky, a place where the water had been touched only by the heavens. The scene was breathtaking. When we arrived, it was quite cloudy, but once the sun started to come out, Don Acho and Doña Susana entered the water to perform blessings upon those who followed them. I was one of the lucky ones to receive this purification of a different kind. I stood barefoot in the freezing lake, with my pant legs rolled up, and Doña Susana stood facing me. Our foreheads were touching as she prayed for me. She sprinkled water on my head at the end as the others watched. And then we hugged and said, "*Aho!*"

After looking down at the bracelet for so long, I finally looked up to see I wasn't alone. Everyone from the retreat had begun to make their way to the circular room. The time had come for us to say goodbye, and Doña Susana would be leading a special ceremony. We entered the main building one by one and made our way around the altar in the center of the room. It was like a massive spiral. The beginning was thousands of rose petals and big fruits like squash and corn; and as the path to the altar got closer to the middle, there were thousands of seeds. The candles of the altar, near the edge, gave the room a soft glow. In silence, we waited.

After a few minutes, Doña Susana entered the room carrying a large crystal bowl. She placed it at the top of the altar, near her feet. "The heart holds secrets. And our hands are the extension of our heart. Water is the master of shape shifting, of transformation, of flow. I want you all to take a candle and rub it all over your body. And while you're doing that, I want you to set an intention." No one hesitated; we all promptly followed her direction. I grabbed the closest candle to me and began rubbing it all over my body. And I thought to myself: "I want to be like water. I want to flow wherever I must go, wherever I am directed to. I want to be of service."

Doña Susana then asked us all to take out the water we had brought from our homes. I had been wondering about the reason for this mysterious task we had all been given beforehand. I had brought water from my two sacred spaces. The first is in the city, at the place where I said goodbye to my brother. It is a place that I still go to often, to feel the veil between worlds. My other space is a little hide-away along the river in the mountains. It is a place that brings me deeper into connection with Mother Earth. "Both of these places are holy to me." I told everyone about the source of my water before I poured it into the crystal bowl. One by one, everyone else did the same, until the bowl was filled with water from around the world. Doña Susana said a prayer to cleanse and bless the water, and then she started to chant. And we all chanted with her. Our chanting filled the air. I never knew any of these sounds could come out of me. Doña Susana then bent down to pick up the crystal bowl and poured the water into a glass pitcher.

She asked us all to place one hand on our hearts and the other on the back of the person next to us and to tell them "I love you." Echoes of "I love you"s filled the room, along with a feeling that something was binding us all together. We all then drank a little bit of the water from the pitcher and began to make our way outside for the second phase of the ceremony.

I could see that Gabriella was guarding the sacred space for the ceremony. We were instructed to wash our feet with lemon and oil before we were allowed to cross the threshold and approach the altar of flowers. I watched everyone at the summit cross that threshold, and the ritual began once everyone had gathered around the altar.

The shamans and their apprentices stood in the middle of the Circle and started to play their drums and other indigenous instruments. I could feel the energy start to expand as the music did, and the drums began to take us on a journey. Susana instructed us to face in all directions and call out to our ancestors to thank them for their sacrifice. We thanked our brothers and sisters in the north, west, south, and east, and then we fell to the ground and put our foreheads on the earth to thank Mother Earth and say a prayer. Doña Susana then walked around with a large feather wand and patted it on our heads and hearts and said a prayer for protection and a prayer to activate our intentions. "We are planting seeds for a new world. So put these seeds in your heart and take care of them. Please use them well."

And then, out of nowhere, we all saw a condor flying over our heads. We were in disbelief, and in a state of reverence for the sighting. To see the most powerful symbol of the shamans' teachings was a clear mark of the finality we were in. There was no going back to who we were, but it was time to make our way back home, carrying the seeds of a new world.

PART TWO

MEXICO CITY

Mexico City sits atop an ancient lake bed that with each passing moment sinks further and further down. The amount of water sourced from this aquifer has created this effect and is irreversible. So Mexico City is sinking. This lake also creates a softness in the soil that amplifies any movements of the tectonic plates beneath it. So, with each passing moment, the moment of truth, the moment of movement, approaches. On September 19, 1985, one of the most powerful earthquakes ever recorded hit Mexico City; the magnitude was 8.1. The energy released was equivalent to 1,114 nuclear weapons exploding. The center of the quake was actually in the Pacific Ocean, so the vibrations were recorded all the way to Los Angeles. The damage was quite extensive to most of the buildings, but one building suffered zero damage. It was the most famous skyscraper in the historic city center. The architect who designed it was actually in the building during the earthquake, on the twenty-fifth floor. He watched all the buildings around him collapse, knowing that he had accomplished something quite outstanding. I can only imagine the feeling he felt. The aftershock hit the next day, and it was incredibly powerful as well—a 7.5 magnitude. And it was in this moment that I was born. At 4:04 a.m. on September 20, in West LA. So I'd like to think that my birth was earth-shattering. But most importantly, I'd like to think that there is something special waiting for me in Mexico City. That the resonance of the Earth, disrupted by the earthquake, is tied to me. And that there's something to be found, and I don't have much time to find it.

Chapter Six

The Heart Knows the Truth

Mexico City, it seems, has been calling me since birth. This day was in the eleventh month of my thirty-fourth year, so visiting Mexico City had taken me awhile, but I planned to make up for it. The plan was to have no plan. Instead, I would go there to explore and see what parts of me I would find there. It had been five months since I had returned from Ecuador, and the divine mission I'd been given was like a beautiful cumulus cloud following me everywhere. I knew that I had to continue my journey with the shamans, but I honestly had no idea how. All I had was the faith that I would, and all I knew was that I was going to Mexico City.

A week before my flight, the pressure started to get to me. I couldn't shake the feeling that I should at least try to find a shaman to have an experience with. I could feel deep in my bones that this book would be about more than one healing practice—that it would be, hopefully, about them all. I knew that wherever I would go in the world, I would gather more and more research to inform the world and more magical experiences to write stories about. So I decided to message Itzhak (the facilitator of the shamanic retreat in Ecuador) to see if he knew anyone. His answer was: "If you ask, you will find." It was a very shamanic answer, so I just did what I knew: Google Search. I typed "shaman, Mexico City" in the search bar, and I found a shamanic retreat that had been organized in Mexico City by a woman who was actually based in Montréal! I knew then that she would be the one who had the answer for me. I just knew that she would know the name of my shaman. And she did. She told me that his name was Miktlan Ehekateotl Kuauhtlinxan, and that she hadn't seen or heard from him in a while, but that he was the one.

I did some research and found out that Miktlan Ehekateotl Kuauhtlinxan is the Carrier of the Eagle Word from the Tetzkatlipoka continuous tradition and a master of the Wewepathli medicine system. He is also the subject of a documentary called *Serpent and the Sun*. I found him on Facebook and messaged him my intentions and my travel plans. He wanted to speak with me on the phone, so we did. I am pretty sure that he just wanted to test me—to know that my intentions were pure. And in the end, I passed the test.

So I would be on my way to Mexico City for the first time, for the most epic adventure. All I could hope was for everything to go according to a plan that I wasn't yet aware of. I guess I had just gotten used to this way of living now, and maybe in some way it had come to define me. I knew that all I could expect was the unexpected.

The unexpected arrived faster than I thought, as I arrived in Mexico City six hours later than I was supposed to. It was around 10 p.m. when I made my way into the taxi. My driver's name was Jose, and I knew that he would be one of my guides in this land. I always feel safe even when traveling alone because I know that, along with heavenly guides, I have earthly ones too. Jose knew exactly what I needed: street tacos. We were a match made in heaven from the start. I was exhausted from the flight, but as soon as we were off to get those tacos, I could feel it. The energy of Mexico is home, is freedom.

The next morning, I was greeted with a beautiful Mexican breakfast in the black-and-white tiled courtyard, and in my glee for all things beautiful (especially breakfast), I opened my phone to record a selfie video for my Instagram. After all, this was a journey I wanted not just to write but to tell visually.

"It's about 7:45, and I am gonna be heading to Teotihuacán, which is the most important pyramid site in Mexico, and is linked to the Giza pyramid in Egypt. The Toltecs, who were before the Aztecs, pre-Aztec, built these pyramids to understand their connection to the Universe. So I'm going to this ancient sacred site today, and I'm also going to meet with a shaman, an Aztec shaman; in Spanish they call them *curanderos*, which means healer. A shaman is someone who not only relates to the physical, human world but also to the elements— to the sun, to the stars, to the spirit world, to Nature—and through that they find balance, unity, and peace. We all have the potential to be shamans; it is in our DNA. This is what the awakening process is; it's activating this in our DNA. And as for me, my mission is to write a book about shamanism, so I'm going to be meeting with shamans from all around the world."

I didn't know I was getting a tour guide; I thought I had only hired a driver. But as soon as I made my way downstairs and entered the corridor, I could see two people in the car. As I got closer, I could see my name in the window: Cherizar Walker. There was an old man sitting on the passenger side wearing aviators and a suit. He saw me then and asked the driver to open the door for me. I slipped into the car excitedly, and the old man introduced himself: "My name is Joaquin, and I'm your guide."

It was the time of day downtown when the streets were completely empty. I love this time. I love when all you can see is how the light dances with the concrete. As we passed through the historic center, Joaquin told me stories about certain buildings and areas. Once we got onto the highway, the conversation transitioned to my reason for being there. I could feel a distinctive peak in his presence when I told him. And suddenly, we were in this together. Suddenly, we were comrades, and he was saving Private Ryan. Suddenly, he had a mission just like me. He told me he knew a famous shaman in the Teotihuacán area and that he would introduce me. He said that Mexicanos referred to shamans as *medico brujos*.[10] I asked him what her name was, and he chuckled: "I have never asked." Well, today, he would get his chance.

As we drove on the highway, Joaquin kept telling me stories. The stories were believable, but I still couldn't believe this situation I was in. We had been on the highway for about twenty minutes, and I kept looking around, contemplating about the wonder of my life. I was surprised to see a cable car fly over my head, so I asked Joaquin about it. This experience reminded me of when I was in Ecuador, 16,000 feet in the sky, when we took a trip to Mama Cotacachi,

---

[10]Witch doctors.

which is what the people of Ecuador call the Cotacachi volcano, one of the oldest in the world. We traveled there as a group to give our praise and thanks to the lands that surrounded us. On our way there, we saw how the villagers in the mountains traveled across the valleys using cable cars. So when I saw this cable car in Mexico City, it immediately took me back to that moment in time. It was the view while I traveled to the sacred lake where I was baptized, and now it is the view as I travel to a sacred place of a different kind.

"The City of the Gods. We have arrived. It is not a coincidence that I have brought you here today." Joaquin spoke these words as we pulled up to the entrance of Teotihuacán. He could've taken the words out of my mouth; the synchronicity was mind-blowing. I mean, I just so happened to book a "driver" who turned out to be a wise man filled with the precise knowledge necessary. Now I was assured that this experience was as much meant for him as it was for me. We drove towards the west side on the Avenue of the Dead, the road encircling the pyramids. We pulled over and got out to take a look from where we were. Through the diamonds of the fencing, I could see a road headed towards the Pyramid of the Sun. Joaquin said, "From here, I can see mathematics, engineering, the arts, all converging into one point. They don't know for sure who built this city or how or why. It's all purely speculation." The mystery of the pyramids enraptured me more than the drama of this fated moment. As we stood on the outside looking in, Joaquin showed me the talisman around his neck. And then, we were ready to go to the home of the healer who had yet to be named.

We drove around to the other side of the pyramids to what looked like a restaurant. I could see that the sign did indeed say *restaurante* and also *temāzcalli*. I was assured that we were at the right place. We got out of the car, and Joaquin walked to the door and knocked loudly. I thought to myself how beautiful the scene looked. The morning sun was shining down, diagonally across the driveway, in front of the potted flowers. And then, a tiny old woman opened the door. She was wearing a long skirt and a yellow blouse, and she had a cast on her left arm. Her energy was very warm. Joaquin told her I was a journalist who wanted to interview her for my book. I am not sure what else he said, but she smiled and was happy to let us inside. We walked in to what was her restaurant and also her home. It was pretty early in the morning, so it was empty. There were many tables in the dining room. We followed her to a table next to the window and sat down. The wall facing me was filled with masks. She asked her sister in the kitchen to bring us some coffee. She told us she had a meeting soon and didn't have much time, so I didn't waste any. I took out my phone to record, and I began to interview a famous healer next to the Pyramid of the Sun. I couldn't believe this was happening, and yet it was. I felt as though I was doing it and watching myself do it simultaneously. This interview was an out-of-body experience that I never asked to have or anticipated.

Interview with Ema Moreno,
November 22, 2019, Teotihuacán, Mexico

Cherizar: What is your full name?

Ema: Ema Ortego Moreno.

Cherizar: Where were you born?

Ema: I was born in San Francisco Mazapa.

Cherizar: Were your mother and father healers?

Ema: My grandmother and my mother. I come from a tradition.

Cherizar: Did you have a choice?

Ema: I liked it. I was born with the desire to learn. And I learned from my grandmother and mother.

Cherizar: So it was deep in your heart, your desire?

Ema: The mind creates illusion, but the heart knows the truth.

Cherizar: What is a curandera?

Ema: A medicine woman.

Cherizar: You use the natural elements.

Ema: Yes. Herbs, stones, flowers, obsidian—the magic crystal. This crystal has the capacity to absorb and contain, maintain the cosmic energy. And with this, I cure people. I give a massage with the obsidian. I take away the negative energy, and I give back the positive energy.

Cherizar: Can you see energy, an aura?

Ema: We have an energy and I use it, but I use my intuition, my feelings. I don't see a color.

THE HEART KNOWS THE TRUTH

Cherizar: Is that how you perform the diagnosis?

Ema: I use different methods depending on the illness. I use eggs, or fire, aromas, flowers. It's according to what the body needs.

Cherizar: Do you do readings?

Ema: No, this is totally different. It's a different method. I use a glass with the ancestral medicine.

Cherizar: Where do you get the medicine?

Ema: It's a family recipe. All the knowledge is in your heart, where all the feelings are.

Cherizar: Do you have a connection to your grandma?

Ema: Only in dreams. They guide me in my dreams.

Cherizar: What things do you do every day, that we can do every day, to grow in this way? To reconnect with our roots?

Ema: Talk to the Universe, the Cosmos. We are a part of the Cosmos. We are energy.

Cherizar: Do you feel the feminine energy is rising in the Cosmos?

Ema: Yes. Women are the ones that maintain the energy. Women are the creators. Mankind hasn't recognized the value of women. And now, there is a world movement. Women are standing up. Women are confusing liberty with rebellion; they have to learn the responsibility and the values of the family. The values are at home. The education is at home. If you have a broken family, there is nothing to be done except love. You have to infuse love with this desire.

I wanted to tell her that maybe rebellion is the right path to liberation, and that maybe there exists a future where women can have it all. I wanted to tell Ema this, but I didn't. I changed the subject.

Cherizar: What do you think cancer is?

Ema: It means they have to work on their emotions. All the bad feelings they have need to be converted into love. Negative emotions are the mother of all the illnesses.

Cherizar: What is temāzcalli?

Ema: The temāzcalli is a temple. The temāzcalli brings out things that are deeply rooted in your body. Using the temāzcalli, people have discovered things that they never knew were inside them.

Cherizar: Do you use plant medicine like Ayahuasca?

Ema: No. I don't use any hallucinogens. We don't need that. These things are not natural. There was a lady from Oaxaca and became famous to use the mushrooms, but she had the ancestral knowledge. You have to have a special knowledge to do this. People use this and become addicts, and that is not good.

Cherizar: Do you eat meat?

Ema: Very little.

Cherizar: Is it unhealthy?

Ema: Yes. I only eat fruits and vegetables and seeds.

Cherizar: Do you drink alcohol?

Ema: No, but I use it to heal the people.

Cherizar: Do you use it to create fire?

Ema: Yes. You spit it on the fire to create the flame.

Cherizar: Yes, I have seen it. Do you use cannabis?

Ema: Yes, I use CBD.

Cherizar: Do you have children?

Ema: No, I never got married. I already had a destiny written by God. I got engaged, but the next step never happened.

Cherizar: Do you have siblings?

Ema: I have nine siblings: seven women and two men.

Cherizar: Are they all healers?

Ema: No, they don't want to. Only me, a brother, a sister, and two nieces are healers.

Cherizar: So your nieces are going to carry on the tradition?

Ema: Yes.

Cherizar: Do you do certain rituals for the new moon or full moon?

Ema: Yes. It depends. I use the four phases of the moon, and for every phase I do a different ritual.

Cherizar: What do you do for the new moon?

Ema: A ritual for strength. I use obsidian and other types of stones.

Cherizar: Is it also a time when you should make intentions?

Ema: Yes, but it takes awhile for it to manifest. It is like waiting for a baby to be born. The full moon is the strongest.

Cherizar: What ritual should we do for the full moon?

Ema: I charge the obsidian with the cosmic energy. I have to wash the stone with sea salt and then put it in water and then put it out at night under the moon.

Cherizar: So what do you see on me? Can you give me a reading?

Ema: You have a very good sense of humor. You love life. You have a strong life energy and creativity. You have very good roots. You have your internal personality, your ego. By practicing your internal lingo, you can call upon your ancestors.

Cherizar: How do I do it?

Ema: It is a discipline. It is work. It is compromise. Everyone has the capacity to be what I am. You have to practice. You have to practice how to breathe, to meditate, to set intentions. You have to see it with your mind. You have to work with your chakras, and the elements: earth, water, fire, air. You have to study your internal lingo, and you have to use the four elements. The elements that are in your body.

I'm not sure what happened or why, but at this point, I just started to cry.

> **Cherizar:** Sorry I'm crying. Sorry I'm emotional.
>
> **Ema:** You have to work your emotions. You are very sensitive lady, yeah? What a sentiment you have.
>
> **Cherizar:** I think it's because this moment is so special, and I feel it and I can't contain it.
>
> **Ema:** You have all the knowledge in your DNA. Intelligence is a machine that brings you to the future and to the past. You have a very strong emotions, and not just now, since you were a child.
>
> **Cherizar:** Yeah, I remember.
>
> **Ema:** Feel, feel it.
>
> **Cherizar:** Yes. These feelings are what brought me here and why I am writing.

Our translator and guide, Joaquin, interrupted for a moment, possibly as overwhelmed as I was: "There is a purpose here. This is not a coincidence. It is why I'm here doing the translation and why your sensitivities are being heightened."

I nodded in approval, and a shiver ran through my body. I looked at how the light poured in through the windows and the sound of someone sweeping in the kitchen. I got lost in the moment.

> **Ema:** How old are you?

Cherizar: Thirty-four.

Ema: You are very young. Are you happy with this moment?

Cherizar: Yes, that is why I am crying.

The real reason I was crying was because of a broken dream. It's like when you have a dream that feels so real that when you wake up, you just want to lie there with your eyes closed to hold on to it. The night I met Emilio was that kind of dream, and when I think about us, it feels like a fairytale that I must know the ending to. So I did something crazy the summer after Ecuador. I woke up one morning, and I finally told him the truth. I told him that I was in love with him.

I didn't just do it out of nowhere. I had actually run into him on the street, as soon as I got back from Ecuador. It had only been two weeks since I had powerful encounters with three different shamans on his birthday, and there he was, the birthday boy, walking across the street in front of me. I saw him walk past the restaurant where I was, and then I saw him turn around for some unknown reason and walk back. It was as if we were magnets, and he was drawn back to me. I called out to him to get his attention, and he walked over towards me. As soon as we were in the vicinity of each other, I felt like I was in another reality. Our connection felt the same as it always had. He was gushing about me in a state of nervousness, but at the same time, something had changed in him. I could feel it.

Ever since then, I knew I couldn't turn away just yet. Instead, I decided to send him a voice message:

"I know it's almost been a year since your mom died from cancer, and I wanted to tell you that the pain doesn't go away. But still somehow, you are made stronger because of it. It gives you the opportunity to turn something painful into your greatest power. And this is why I am sending you this message. The last time I saw you, you seemed so sad, like you really needed me to tell you something. So here I am, telling you how I feel once and for all. I am crazy about you, Emilio. I think about you all the time. I can't pretend to conceive of the reason why, but I know I was meant to tell you: that I am in love with you."

I honestly thought I would never hear from him again after sending this message, and to be honest, I wish I never did. When I finally heard back from him, he said that the reason he had been so distant towards me was that he had gotten back together with his ex. My heart was shattered. It is a pain I wouldn't wish on anyone.

I told Ema the real reason I was so emotional was that I loved a man who didn't love me back. I asked her if she had ever been in love. She smiled. I could tell by her lack of a response that true love was just not in the cards for her. I changed the subject.

> **Cherizar:** Do you feel like the world is changing right now? That we're entering a new age?

> **Ema:** The planet is changing, but the humans are going down.

> **Cherizar:** But some of us are being awakened, right?

> **Ema:** Yes . . . but there are babies that are not educated and don't have mothers. And there are a lot of young people with a nice vision, but they can't do anything.

Cherizar: What advice would you give to the world? To heal themselves?

Ema: We have to recognize our roots. To know ourselves in this way.

Cherizar: Do you meditate or pray?

Ema: Yes, it is a good way to release.

Cherizar: Do you have a special place to meditate?

Ema: I have an altar at my house. But any place is sacred; it is all under the Cosmos. Any place is sacred.

Cherizar: So why is the pyramid special?

Ema: They are energy. Energy of the Earth.

Cherizar: How do you think they were built?

Ema: Nobody knows except the ancient people. And they were very advanced.

Cherizar: Have you ever had an out-of-body experience or something you can't explain?

Ema: Only once in my life. I got lost one time. I was on a bus and felt like my soul came out of my body. I felt like I was in another dimension. It was only two minutes. I couldn't understand what had happened. I tried to analyze the situation, but I couldn't understand it. This place has energy because of the pyramids.

Her last sentence seemed out of place. I don't know if it was the translation, or if she felt the experience was caused by the pyramids.

In any case, the pyramids would be our next stop, so perhaps this sentence was perfectly in place. After the interview, we headed outside. I wanted to take her picture, and I wanted to take it in front of her home and healing space. So after we said our thank yous and goodbyes, I took a picture of Ema Ortega Moreno, the famous healer from Teotihuacán.

Chapter Seven

You Are the Universe

The beauty of Juan Gabriel's voice graced the sonic frequencies as we went nowhere fast. I was with my guide, Jose, and we were stuck in Mexico City traffic, headed towards the hills of Morales. We were almost out of the city, finally making headway to meet Miktlan. Jose was showing me this performance of Juan Gabriel at the Palacio Nacional, where he's strutting like James Brown in front of this massive line of mariachis. We were watching it on YouTube, and I couldn't believe I had never seen it. The performance was like Pavarotti singing "Nessum Dorma" or Beyoncé at Coachella. The scene was no doubt the epitome of how music connects us to the Divine. We were surrounded by thousands of people and honking cars, but I was at peace. Jose was the driver to our destination, and I was the passenger finding silence amid the chaos. I looked at myself in the rearview mirror and thought back to another chapter in my adventures in Mexico, when I was also the passenger.

In another part of Mexico, in a different dimension of time, I popped open a can of beer and handed it to my fiancé. We had just got engaged and were headed to Chichen Itza. Bruno and I both had an obsession with Mexico, so whenever I'm here, I can't help but think about how this was our happy place. It was where we got engaged, and where we walked the streets of Merida to celebrate and then drove to Celestún where the flamingos flock and watched the most beautiful sunset ever. We drove all over the Yucatan to see the pyramids and the cenotes, and I got carsick at one point. At one cenote we found ourselves alone, so we got naked and jumped in. We had the most epic adventures from the very start, and at the same time maybe simultaneously, we had the most epic fights. I suppose this was our fate. In one moment, we could understand each other at a cellular level, and in another moment have no understanding of each other at all. We would fight up close, but it seemed as though we were miles away—an entire universe from reconciliation. I can't recall fighting while in Mexico though. This place was sacred to us. Perhaps our residence in another life.

Looking back, I realize being on the road made us happy; we just didn't do it enough. One time we drove across the country together. He drove and I read *On the Road* by Jack Kerouac out loud—a symbolic act we were both into. It was as if we had this reverence for a certain feeling and had to feel it.

Years later we would take that Bob Dylan feeling and sing songs together. Bruno would play the guitar, and we would sing love songs and sad ones too. All the best parts stuck around until the end, but in the end even the best couldn't save us from the truth. In the end

I had to break it off so we didn't end up hating each other. I wrote him a letter: "Dear B., 7 reasons why we can't be." And that was it. Seven years to the day after we had fallen in love in September. It's crazy because I realize now that our last conversation was the kind of conversation we had always fought to have but never could. And the relationship we have now is the relationship we had always been fighting for. We are no longer together, but we are more together than ever. We made it.

Objects in the mirror are closer than they appear. I read this as we finally made it out of the city and into the hills of Morales. I couldn't stop staring at this phrase on the side mirror and thinking about the deeper meaning of the expression. I always found it to be so interesting, almost like a riddle. And the synchronicity in this moment was killing me. The moment that was destined was getting closer and closer as we drove deeper into the hills. We exited the highway at a sign that said *Tres Marías*. We had arrived.

It was a rural town, so the roads were a bit bumpy. We drove past a few farms first and then entered a residential neighborhood. I could immediately tell which gate was Miktlan's. It was the only black one on a street full of white ones. I texted him to let him know that we were outside. A few minutes later, he came out to greet us. He was wearing all black, and his long hair was tied in a low ponytail. He wore round glasses. His dogs also came to greet me, and they nipped at my heels. He yelled, "*Abajo!*" as I followed him onto his property. I could see his house towards the left, and I could see apple trees and what were surely lots of medicinal plants. There were also a few animal pens. It was obviously a farm, but he didn't have any animals except his dogs.

As I followed him further, I immediately began to trust him and this whole experience. I felt an immediate softness with him, as if we were already friends. His house looked to me like a solarium for some reason. I'm not sure why but maybe it was how the light shone through the windows. I could just tell that his house had a way of capturing the sun. He took me into the back room because he said he had been cleaning in the front. He asked me if I wanted water, and I declined. I sat down on a straw chair, and he sat down on one in front of me. It wouldn't be long before the day became night, so we didn't waste any time starting our sacred dialogue.

"You didn't send me a letter," a scolding by Miktlan to begin the dialogue.

"I will."

"Usually I don't give interviews if I don't have this letter. Forty years ago we started to have this way to ask people to give us their intentions before we give interviews. It is important for us."

"It is for the Council?"

"Yes. Because people use the information in a bad way, and we don't like this."

"Okay, well, here is my letter for you:

"My name is Cherizar Walker. I am a writer. I have been writing about my spiritual journey, about my awakening, for some time. Writing for me is one of the main modalities for healing. As I walked on this path, I have discovered more of what my purpose is. Last year though, I was given a huge task by the Divine. I had a feeling and I sought a guidance, and this very wise man who sees told me I was destined to write a book that would bridge the old shamanism to the new in a most profound way. After that, I traveled to Ecuador and had encounters with the Incan shamans and learned their ways. And now, I have found you in the most serendipitous way. My intention in coming to you is to share your wisdom and your message with this dying world in hopes of conceiving of a new one. I come with a pure heart and soul."

English was not his first language and I talk fast, so I wasn't sure if he caught all of that. After I said it, his response was just to make sure that I would send whatever I wrote to him beforehand. So I confirmed to him again and continued to explain myself:

"I am writing from my heart. It is not just about my experiences, but about my feelings, my everything. But I will write exactly what you say."

"I know you are coming with your heart, but these words are important to be signed off on, if we wish to share our message with the world."

"I completely understand."

Interview with Miktlan Ehekateotl, November 22, 2019, Tres Marías, Morelos, Mexico

Cherizar: Guys like Carlos Castaneda—you know him? Or do you know his master, Don Juan?

Miktlan: Yes, he died a few years ago.

Cherizar: Have you read his book, Carlos Castaneda?

Miktlan: Yes, well, I opened the book and read the first words, and I thought that this is not Toltec. I am not sure about this person. And I have spoken to other people who he supposedly worked with, and they said that the things he had said about them weren't true. That he wasn't where he said he was.

Cherizar: Yeah, well, it's a fiction, but some of the wisdom is nice.

Miktlan: It's okay.

Cherizar: What he talks about, how Death is your greatest advisor in your life, for you to understand your mortality. Stuff like that I liked.

Miktlan: Yeah, I respect what he did, but it depends on the reader what they will do with it. So what do you want to know?

Cherizar: I want to know about your journey to being who you are today. Where were you born? Was it in your family? Did you have a period when you did not want this path? Like, your whole journey.

Miktlan: Okay. Well, I was born in a Mexican family. My father is from the tradition that I practice. It is called Tetzkatlipoka tradition. This tradition is called continuous because it's passed throughout the generations. It is not tied to an ethnic group; it is from this area of Mexico, the center. This tradition has been influenced by many cultures like the Toltecs and Aztecs and Mazatecs. We are not the only one tradition. We have four traditions, and we are the smallest group. I had the fortune through my father to learn this tradition; it's called Wewepathli. For a long time, we couldn't show who we are.

Cherizar: Why?

Miktlan: When the Spanish arrived in 1531, we decided to hide our tradition for our safety. Because they persecuted these traditions and tried to kill those who carried the wisdom. We teach the full knowledge on the men's side. Because women get married and might marry a Christian, and she may tell her husband about us and may put us at risk. And that is why we teach only the practices to the women, but not the cosmology. Only if the women decide to not get married, we are open to her. So in my family. We are four: two sisters and two brothers. And only the brothers received the Word.

Cherizar: So, since you were little, you watched your dad do healings?

Miktlan: Well, everyone knew my dad did healings. But they did not know that we were from a specific tradition. My father had his own business and carried a briefcase. And with this briefcase he could put food on the table. But the service of the medicine is only for trusted people. We had some rooms where he would speak the language, the Nahuatl[11] language, but we couldn't speak the Nahuatl language outside the home. The treatments done outside the house, outside the ceremonial room, were conducted in Spanish. My sisters didn't learn how to speak Nahuatl.

Cherizar: Would you watch him do healings?

---

[11] The language of the Aztec and Nahua peoples, which is still spoken in some parts of Mexico today.

Miktlan: It's not only healings. But it's a full tradition. The knowledge is not only medicine. The knowledge is about the culture. It is about the construction, astronomy. It is a full tradition. The healings are only one part; it is not the principal thing. But on the other side, it is a principal thing that we have to know to heal ourselves and stay healthy. So in Spanish we call it *Limpia*.

Cherizar: Okay, so what do you call yourself? *Brujo*, no? (We laugh.)

Miktlan: No. Let me answer your questions because you have asked me a few.

I learned from my father since I was thirteen, and then I decided to not live with him because I felt pushed towards the tradition. So I told my parents, "Sorry, but I'm leaving because I need to experience other things. Thank you so much." They said, "Okay, son, when you want to return, this is your house." So I went and had my own experience with different traditions, but something wouldn't let me go. If I heard about a ceremony from my tradition was taking place or something, I would feel like I had to be there. I felt like I had to go. And I would go in secret, so my father wouldn't know. Now I understand it was because I am a reflection of my father, and I couldn't escape from this even though I tried.

Cherizar: Do you do other things other than heal?

Miktlan: Yes, it's important that we have normal jobs for balance. We do healings and receive gratifications, but with that it's not enough for you to have an economic balance. So we have to have another business. In fact, in my generation, all my cousins went to university. So we have to live two lives—normal life and the traditional life. This is important because we are still living in the land where we are building our city, where we are one of the families to form this city, and to practice this tradition for the last 698 years. And we were born here. Only in the next generation, our grandchildren started to be born outside of Mexico City.

Cherizar: But you were born in Mexico City?

Miktlan: Yes, I was born in Mexico City, where my father was born.

Cherizar: You live in the city?

Miktlan: No, I live here. But this is just an address. I live here (and he pointed to his heart). I go to the city frequently because the people are there and we are their healers.

Cherizar: So you have a house there?

Miktlan: It's my family house. I go there in the day, but I come here by the end of the day because I am working on the land.

Cherizar: But do you feel better here?

I was trying to lead him into explaining why he lived in these mountains.

Miktlan: I feel good anywhere. I live here (and he pointed to his heart). The place is only a context. I feel good everywhere: in the city, in the mountains, at the beach. It's not important where I am; it's important what I do with myself.

Not what I do with another person. How I enjoy my life. We are here not for crying, but for enjoying. And to share your life with those around us. You can see my dogs. But they are not my dogs; they are my friends. And they make me happy. But I protect them, and they protect me, and we protect us. If someone were to jump over the wall, they would certainly start barking to control them, not to attack, to control. Only if I tell them to attack. But I'm not going to do that unless it's something dangerous.

One day a kid's ball came over the wall. And this day I was in the field in the back. And I hear the dogs barking, and I came and the kid is in the corner, and the dogs are cornering him. And I ask him: "Who are you?" And he said that his ball came into the yard, and he knocked on the door, and no one answered.

We are human beings. If you have a disagreement with me, maybe you will attack me, but before I respond I will try to speak to you, even if you are attacking me with a machete. But maybe I will have to defend myself and I will cut your head off. But it will be without any animosity or any anger. My heart has to be clean. In our tradition, if you have to cut the head, it is in defense. It is a warrior's tradition, but the war is because we disagree with someone. The battlefield is where we can balance our energies. Even if you have the biggest army, a small group of people can control you. They can put you down. So it's important that we are not extremely proud of these things.

Do you want to take a walk?

Cherizar: Sure, it's nice outside. I see you have cherry blossoms.

We got up and began to walk outside in the fields.

Cherizar: So you were saying that you were trying to go to the ceremonies in secret, because you were too proud.

Miktlan: Yes, when I was seventeen, and after I had studied a few other traditions, I did not feel a connection to the other traditions. The only one that made me feel a connection was this. So in that case, I returned to my father and asked if he could continue his teachings with me. And he said, "No, you have to go to the Council, and they have to accept you for you to continue the tradition." So I went to them, and they sent me to a teacher to learn from.

Cherizar: So what was the learning? What did you have to do? You were an apprentice?

Miktlan: We are apprentices all of our lives. After my parents, I studied with twenty-two masters.

Cherizar: You studied with twenty-two masters?!

Miktlan: Yes, because I learned about different things. The different ceremonies, the dances. It is more doing than talking.

He stopped then to pick up a plant to show me.

This plant, this yellowish bulb, is not poisonous for the Mexican native people. But for the rest of the people, it is poison!

Cherizar: So there is something in your genes?

Miktlan: Yes exactly.

The sun was making its way to the other side of the world then and leaving us here in darkness. Miktlan walked in front of me, in the high grass, as the light disappeared from the sky.

> **Miktlan:** In our tradition, the body is divided into four parts: the physical body, the mental body, the emotional body, and what we call the tonal body. The tonal is not exactly the same as spirit, but spirit is part of the tonal. The spirit is this side, and the tonal is the other side.

> **Cherizar:** Tonal, as in vibrations?

> **Miktlan:** Yes, it is a part of the bio atmosphere you have in your body. This bio atmosphere is bioelectric. This bio electromagnetism is like your computer's hard drive. This is where it is holding all of your experiences since you were born, until now. And these memories are the memory of your computer. But at the same time, you have elements of consciousness. These four parts are not you; you are your soul. And our soul connects to your body through the anima. This is like your Wi-Fi connection. And you are on your computer writing, and this is your avatar. It's like when you play video games and you have to decide on which superhero you are. And you design it. You decide. Well, it's exactly the same with yourself. What is the personality you want? Even the body; your body is designed by yourself.

> **Cherizar:** So you are saying that we design ourselves?

> **Miktlan:** Yes, and at the same time, we decide how to use our avatar in this world. These decisions are more the

spiritual things. It's more than deciding where you travel or if you want a dog.

Cherizar: But what about this connection? For most people, is there something wrong with this connection?

Miktlan: Yes.

He picked up a plant and began to explain its uses.

Miktlan: This herb can treat infections in your stomach, in your lung, in your liver, in different parts. Now it is the season for this. So we are gathering the plants and preparing them using the fertilization by animals.

Cherizar: So back to the disconnection from our spirit. Is that another part of your tradition?

Miktlan: Yes, we work to reconnect the physical body with the mental body. The mental body is not thinking; it is the nervous system: the central nervous system and your brain. This part is only the wires, but with the memory, we decide. The most important body is the tonal. We perceive the physical most easily, but not as much as we perceive the tonal. When we pay too much attention to the physical, we lose the connection with the other three. Sometimes we pay attention to our emotions when we are scared and feel our emotions. Most of the sicknesses come from emotions, depending on how you experience life.

We are like laboratory rats. If you are given red candy and you enjoy this red candy, and the scientist takes back the red candy and slaps you, you will have the memory for the rest of your life that this candy is *no bueno*. These kinds of memories [are] how you are building yourself. And that is related to your emotions. Because in that instance we felt something we didn't like. You can call it a trauma.

Cherizar: So a lot of our illness comes from our emotional body?

Miktlan: Yes, most of the sickness comes from your emotions. It is useful when you express your love to somebody. And if you bring your hand to your heart. If that person broke your heart, you say that he broke your heart. But if you study the gorillas, in the jungle, they bang their hand on their chest to indicate that you are a friend. And if he wants to communicate that you are not welcome, he will bang on his chest the same. It's exactly the same! *Ya no quiero y yo quiero est la mema.* It's emotions.

You can eat that plant and maybe it will make you sick, and I could eat that plant and maybe it won't make me sick. We have memories in our bodies—memories of all the generations past. Because maybe at some point my tribe had to eat these plants to survive. And they survived. And that gave me some defense.

Cherizar: Are you saying that our memories are tied to our ancestors' traumas as well? That their trauma is ours as well?

Miktlan: Yes, but not all of their trauma. Let me tell you something. All the memories of your father and all the memories of your mother come to you by your genes, and everything your father lived before your conception is passed to you like a memory, and every memory from your mother, when you are in her womb and if she breastfeeds you, all her experience passes to you too. After that, maybe they will pass to you habits because you watched them, but the important part is in the DNA. It's the ancestral memories.

I remember one day I was painting a house, and it was an old house, and the sink faucet was broken. And I thought that it needed a plastic O-ring. But when I opened it, I could see that it was designed before that—that it was very old and I didn't know what to do. And immediately it came to my mind to get a cotton rope with a wax and to make a spiral in the faucet, and I put it there and it fixed it. Why did this memory come? Because my grandfather from my mother's side was a plumber. I never worked with him; I was four or five when he died. But that memory came from him.

I went to my uncle who was a plumber, and I asked him how he would fix that problem, and he explained you have to have a cordon and put on the wax in a spiral way.

Cherizar: Wow.

Miktlan: It's not only me. You could do something and not know where it's coming from. These are the memories of your ancestors, and it only comes out when you need it. In my tradition we say the problems are not a problem, but a challenge to your mind, to your knowledge. And if you recognize all your body, all the particles of your body [come] from the beginning of the Universe, and [have] the memory of all the experience of the Universe, you can only conclude that *you are the universe*. Your perception of the universe is a result of the problems you have in front of you. You are supported through all the knowledge in the Universe, though, so you don't need to ask anyone. If the problem is there, it's because you can solve it.

Cherizar: So the work that we do is to allow us to access that knowledge. So we unblock the things that block us from that access?

Miktlan: Yes, exactly. Why? Because in history we have been controlled by religions, by governments, by the nation, by the society, and they limit you and make you think that you can't solve anything. My tradition is not a religion. It is a way of life. You see I can smoke; I can have a mezcal or drink a coffee.

Cherizar: A little bit.

Miktlan: Exactly. My father told me if you want to drink alcohol, drink the cup; don't let the cup drink you. If you want to smoke, smoke and enjoy, but don't let the cigarette and the tobacco smoke you.

Cherizar: But you use the smoke in your healings, as a protection, right?

Miktlan: It's not a protection. It is a way to clean.

I asked him if the cigarettes were made from pure tobacco. He told me that it was the purest in the region. So I asked him for a cigarette.

Cherizar: I don't smoke, but I want to try. So when you do healings, do you wear something for protection?

Miktlan: Now, no; but in the past, yes. I had to teach my body first. But now I don't need to.

I lit the cigarette, and he told me not to let the smoke get to my lungs, just in the mouth.

> **Miktlan:** We say white people are sick from the tobacco because they don't know how to smoke it.

> **Cherizar:** But it's also the diet.

> **Miktlan:** No, it's not just the diet. It's more than the diet; it's the emotions. The emotions you have make you sick.

> **Cherizar:** But even good emotions? Or just bad emotions? From my understanding, love is the only digestible emotion.

> **Miktlan:** No. You can call it love. In my language they don't really have a word for *love*. We have something similar, but it's not exactly love. It's *tlazotlas;* it means "earth flowing to the earth." If I have a partner or when I talk to my children, I use this word. This is the closest to *love*.

> **Cherizar:** Beautiful. Have you ever been in love?

> **Miktlan:** Yes. I have been in love with somebody. I would say, "*Ni mítz tlazotlas*"; it means "I am flowing the earth to you." It is a correspondence. I have another word too, but I do not remember. Between the Spanish, English, and Nahuatl, it's difficult to find the words.

> **Cherizar:** It's okay; it will come to you. So you don't say "*Te amo*"?

> **Miktlan:** For a long time, if someone said "*Te amo*," I felt weird. It's because in my language, when we say "No," we say "*Te amo*," so in my language *te amo* is "you not."

Cherizar: Oh wow! That's funny.

Miktlan: I don't know how many loves I lost because of that. But only six years ago, I noticed this. That is the point. If someone tells me, I understand because you can transform your experience.

Cherizar: Yes, because love is not a word; it's a feeling.

Miktlan: Yes, it's a feeling, and it's an action. You don't even need to say anything.

Cherizar: But language is powerful too; words are powerful.

Miktlan: Yes. But they can tell you something that is not true. You have to check to see if the other person feels the same. It's a cycle. It has to go both ways.

Cherizar: Do you believe in soul mates? Like our souls were together in a past life?

Miktlan: Okay, could be. It's not only the soul. It's the formulation. It's the chemistry. Do you like coffee?

Cherizar: Yes.

Miktlan: If you go to the coffee shop near to your house and if you prepare at your house, it's a coffee. If you go to Italy to drink a coffee, it's more or less the same. It has a different taste or intensity, but it's a coffee. If I offer you a tea, a green tea, and I tell you this is coffee, you will say, "No, this is tea." It's more or less the same with the humans. Some of us are herbal tea from the mountains; some of us are a coffee. When you find something that is similar in the taste, it's when you notice this connection with that person.

Cherizar: Have you experienced this?

Miktlan: Yes. Everybody who has lived life has felt this. And you can enjoy these flavors in life. And one of the experiences we have for teaching the apprentices is they have to smell the people, and to smell if they have fear, happiness, love . . .

Cherizar: So you can do that?

Miktlan: Yes.

Cherizar: So what about me?

Miktlan: Aaahhhhhhh.

Cherizar: Come on! [We both laugh.]

Miktlan: Later, or maybe next time.

Cherizar: Okay. For sure.

Miktlan: So the experience of being human is how we can find balance, and it's easy to find this for a normal life. If you enter a business meeting and you smell acidity, and they want your money or knowledge, you can smell that. You can know how they react to you. But when you feel comfortable, you can make a business really easy. And that applies not just for business [but also] for relationships.

In order to have a good relationship, you need four things. The first one is the most important—is confidence. If you don't feel confidence, and the guy tries to make a move, you feel that, and you don't need to have training for that. The second one is we have to keep the confidence; we have to improve the confidence with honesty. If you are not honest, the confidence is gone. After that, you have to have respect. You can be honest, but with respect. Speak the truth with respect. And the most important is you have to have a connection with that person. This person has to have something you want. And you have to have something they want. If I try to sell you sweets, and you feel confidence from me, and I am honest with you, and I respect you, and if you want to buy sweets, and I say $100 each, you say, "No, thank you." But if I give a good price, and you agree, and you say, "Okay, I will take one." And this is complete. Any relationship has to have these things. You asked me about my tradition for your book, but I want to share my tradition's way of life. We are clear. We are honest. I feel your intentions are true. You can pass.

You can't really know what I do without experiencing it. So I invite you to the other room for a healing.

I was excited to hear this. I hadn't expected a healing session when I arrived, but Miktlan was right; it would be the best way for me to understand their healing tradition.

I followed him to a separate little house on his property. Inside there was a massage table, a bathroom, and a kitchenette. He told me to lie on the table, and he started to feel different parts of my body. He pushed and prodded me; he pulled my leg and stretched my back. It was part diagnostic and part therapeutic. He started to assess the type of diet I had. He said that I am not eating a lot of meat, which is good, and that everything feels fine. He finished the treatment, which was a type of acupressure massage, and then he covered me up with blankets. He then turned off the lights and left me alone in the little house. I don't know how long I lay there, but I could feel the spirits all around me. And once I really started to get into it, once I started to feel the high vibrations more acutely, he came back.

He asked me how I felt, and I told him that I was just starting to feel it. We laughed as he led me out of the house. It was pitch black by then, so he walked me to the gate. I was happy about everything, and I could tell he was too. The encounter was everything it was meant to be. After we hugged, I promised that I'd be back.

When I got outside of the gate, I was relieved to see that Jose's car was still there. For a moment, I thought that maybe something had gone wrong. For a moment, I thought that this day couldn't end without some form of mishap. It was too perfect so far. But there was Jose, sleeping in the car, patiently waiting for me. I had trusted a stranger in a foreign country with my life that day, and I was blessed. As we drove back, I kept counting my blessings until I could see the lights of the city in the distance. We were almost there, and I couldn't wait to go to sleep. As we got closer to the city, I could see that there was a toll booth at the county line. I opened my purse to get some cash, but there was none; I had used the rest of it to buy us lunch. I was sure though that Jose had cash. I was sure that he had thought about the toll and would have the money, but once we pulled up to the line of cars at the gate, he said that he didn't have any money. I didn't panic. I was sure that they would let us through with a ticket for the fine or that I could pay with a credit card, but once we got to the payment booth, the attendant said we could do neither of those things. I couldn't believe it: we were stranded on the outskirts of Mexico City with no way of getting back in. We both started to laugh then, for that was all we could do. Jose and I laughed and laughed as he backed up his car onto the roadside. After we sat for a moment, he got out of the car and started approaching people in their cars to ask them for money. He came back after a few minutes with enough money for the toll. I let out a big sigh of relief and laughed.

Later on that night after I had just settled into bed, I received a message from Miktlan. The message said, "I just remembered the translation of the word *love* in Nahuatl. It is *tlatzohtla*. It means 'reciprocity.'" My heart lit up. It was the perfect ending to one of the most beautiful days of my life.

Chapter Eight

The Place of the Dead

I never understood the idea of being buried in a coffin. I want to be buried in the dirt when I die. I want to be buried in an unmarked grave in an unknown place in the wild. In the nothingness I will be set free.

Everything has changed so suddenly in my life. It's so terrifying and yet so invigorating. It's like, finally, something is happening. Finally, the visions I see have a place in my reality. Just a few months earlier, I was watching Alfonso Cuarón's cinematic portrayal of his childhood, and now I am living it. I have been walking the streets of Roma the entire morning, seeing in color what Cuarón had painted in black and white. Seeing in real life the magic of his Utopia. It is January 2020, and I have returned to Mexico City, earlier than expected. I don't know why, but I felt this sense of urgency for some reason. Something told me that there was a small window of opportunity to complete what I had started with Miktlan Ehekateotl.

Roma is an intersection of worlds. It is the perfect neighborhood to continue my love affair with Mexico. It has the richness of Art Nouveau next to the aroma of a taco truck—everything required for happiness.

Last time I was here I visited the ancient pyramids of Teotihuacán. I will never forget my arrival at 11:11 on 11/22. When I got to the top, I felt as if I had jumped into a different timeline. Two girls wanted to take a picture with me for some reason, perhaps because they saw something in me that I could yet not see. I posted the picture we took on my Instagram stories, and a random follower I had never spoken to told me something really bizarre: he said that next time I go back to Mexico City, I should do a temāzcalli. I thought to myself: "Who does this guy think he is? Telling me what to do." But after a few minutes, I realized that this was no ordinary stranger and that this was no ordinary message. I knew that when I returned, I had to do the sweat lodge again.

In Ecuador, I felt like I didn't fully commit to the process, like I didn't fully surrender. This time, I had no idea how Miktlan would guide me through the ceremony or who would join me, and I didn't ask him. With such mystery, I would have no choice but to surrender. All Miktlan told me was that I would be picked up by his friend, Wewe, at 1 p.m. in Roma.

By 1:07, Wewe still hadn't arrived, so I decided to message him. And as I did, my phone started to ring; it was him; we were in sync. I ran out to greet Wewe and hopped into the car. I looked at my phone; it was 1:11. The estimated time of arrival on Waze was 3:33. Repeating numbers had been a theme for a while, but it had gotten more intense since my first meeting with Miktlan. I wonder if it will ever stop.

Wewe was quite talkative from the start. He told me about the sun dance performed for the equinox, where they dance all day with no food and water. They just dance for twenty-four hours straight. He told me that he met Miktlan thirty years ago, when he was studying video production. He told me about the mountains we approached, the Ajusco, the sacred land of volcanoes. He told me how Mexico City used to be an island, and how every year it sinks deeper and deeper to its watery roots. And as we crossed into the next state of Morelos, he told me about pulque,[12] which the Aztecs named the "drink of the Gods." I told him about how I was intuitively guided to Miktlan and that because it was so easy, it must be meant to be. He agreed. I told him that I was writing a book on shamanism and conducting research on various traditions from around the world. I told him my next stop was El Transito, Nicaragua.

We arrived at Miktlan's house before 3:33, and the sun was bright. I felt a distinctive energy profile here, so I made a mental note to ask him if there was an energy vortex in these hills. His dogs greeted me first—the keepers of the land. And then I saw Miktlan, Keeper of the Word. He was wearing all black clothing again, but this time, he was wearing a necklace of blue skulls. He was warm and inviting, and we hugged. It was so nice to see my friend again.

As soon as we got to his front door, my eyes were immediately drawn to a large photograph above his couch. It was a photo of a woman in a green dress, holding a black hat over her face. It reminded

---

[12]Alcohol traditional to central Mexico, which is made by fermenting agave sap.

me of a picture of me. I always wonder if there's some deeper meaning to what I'm drawn to or if it just happens. I stared at the woman in the green dress as she lingered on the edge of darkness; I took a picture of her. This time around I saw things that I didn't notice before. I noticed Miktlan had some type of plant or grass above his door, a marking for protection. I noticed the art he had collected over the years. I felt more at home here this time around.

Miktlan asked me if I wanted to go see the temāzcalli, and I said, "Yes, of course," so he took me to where he had built them. There were two: a large one and a small one. I had expected to do the ceremony with Miktlan sitting with me in the temāzcalli, but I guess that wasn't going to happen. He had built a large structure for another group he would be leading, and he had built a smaller structure for me. It looked like a tomb. I told him how it reminded me about something I read in a book about burying oneself for power and enlightenment. The symbolism was so powerful, and it was scary. And I was scared. I was scared I wouldn't make it through the temāzcalli ritual this time.

We walked back inside the house and sat down on the chairs we had sat on two months prior. There was a group of bees next to me buzzing really loudly. Before I could turn on my recorder, Miktlan started to tell me a story about a woman he had been with a long time ago. He wouldn't tell me how long because he wouldn't reveal to me his age. He said that they had a two-month-old at the time, and one night, she told him that she had never experienced someone in her family dying, and she asked him about the experience. The very next morning, their two-month-old daughter passed away from SIDS.

I told him that I was sorry to hear this story. How incredibly ironic life is sometimes.

Interview with Miktlan Ehekateotl, January 17, 2020, Tres Marías, Morelos, Mexico City

Cherizar: My mom always tells me that you are never too old to be taught a lesson from God. Never too old. If you won't tell me your age, tell me your month and day of birth.

Miktlan: The twenty-eighth of March. In my tradition, I am exactly in between the Eagle and the Serpent.

Cherizar: So you are on the cusp. In the zodiac, you are an Aries.

Miktlan: Yes.

Cherizar: How many children do you have?

Miktlan: Thirteen.

Cherizar: [laughing] Are you passing the tradition on to your sons?

Miktlan: Yes, my son who is nineteen wants to study, but he is not yet ready.

Cherizar: Will the tradition be lost if you die?

Miktlan: No, there are others who will continue the traditions.

Cherizar: So what does it mean to be the "Keeper of the Word"?

Miktlan: It's a charge. It's a duty. The President of the United States is the first, but there is Vice President; they are second. It's like that.

Cherizar: Why do you live here? Is there something special about this place?

Miktlan: The place has a special energy, and it is good for my work. It helps me to rest more. In the city I sleep two to three hours; here I can sleep six hours.

Cherizar: So there are places that are more special, that are better for energy?

Miktlan: Yes. Because in Mexico City I was living in an apartment building, and I couldn't fall asleep until 4:00 in the morning because I felt all of their energy, all of their stress, and everything. And so, it was not easy to rest there. Here it is easier. I don't have to feel the energy of everyone around me.

Cherizar: Do you think people should live in places like this (the mountains) versus the city?

Miktlan: Yes.

Cherizar: So tell me about Teotihuacán. What do they teach you about the pyramids?

Miktlan: It was a natural social experiment that was trying to find the balance of the society with the environment. The experiment of Teotihuacán is a very good one; it is not perfect. It was broken by the climate change in that time. They had a dry spell, and the culture was gone. But before that it was a cosmopolitan society. The Toltecs, the Mayans, the

Zapotecs, and we know that other cultures as well visited this place when it was bustling, before the Spanish came. They tried to make society better. They made a mistake by putting a lot of trees around the city, and this dried up the lake.

Cherizar: And you come from the Toltecs?

Miktlan: I come from the Aztec. The Toltec people came before the Aztec. They took a long trip around the continent, and when they returned, their tradition was over; the Aztecs had arrived in the fourteenth century.

Cherizar: Are there still Toltec people alive?

Miktlan: A little bit. The culture is nearly lost.

Cherizar: What do you do at the pyramids?

Miktlan: We have a ceremony there for the spring equinox. The idea is to make an observation about what happened in the environment, in the cosmos and everything. And then we do a calculation for our agriculture and society.

Cherizar: So you make adjustments to align with what's happening cosmically?

Miktlan: Yes, but it's not astrology. It's astronomy—between how the Earth moves in relation to the moon, for example. There is a woman who asks me to write an article four times a year, something short, about the influence of the moon over human beings. For example, if you could take the hair for the new moon, it will grow slow but strong; and for the full moon, it will grow fast but slim. If you want to pick fruit, the best time is during the full moon. But for the new moon, all the nutrients are in the root vegetables.

Cherizar: Is menstrual blood ever used in your moon ceremonies?

Miktlan: Yes, but this work would be facilitated by women. For a cacao ceremony, the women should not have sex for fifteen days, and it is best for virgins to make the cacao. The hormones of the women make it better.

In the past, tobacco was only rolled by virgin women, and it was rolled using the legs.

The hormones make the flavor of the food too. Every meal you cook, you pass your hormones to the food. Every meal will then have a different flavor, based on the ingredients and who has prepared it.

Cherizar: Is this how you choose which places to eat at?

Miktlan: Yes, I smell and feel the energy of the person cooking. The other day I went to see a woman who doesn't smoke and lives alone. We were chatting in her house, and at some point I told her that I know you don't smoke, but I can smell it. She was surprised. Someone had smoked there three weeks ago. I could feel this.

Cherizar: But your senses are better than most people.

Miktlan: Anyone can do it. You just have to pay attention. We just don't pay attention to these things, and we don't have the training to process the situation.

Cherizar: How do we train ourselves to do this?

Miktlan: Do the little things that test the theories of our senses. Pay attention to how you respond to the minute details; this is the magic. The magic is someone who can make something different that people don't understand. The magic is about paying attention.

Cherizar: Is cooking magic?

Miktlan: Yes, we say, "Healing starts in the kitchen."

Cherizar: What is the best diet?

Miktlan: It's about balance and having things from all the different food groups. Lots of fruits, vegetables, roots, lentils, seeds, potatoes, and a tiny bit of meat. You don't have to eat a lot of meat or a ton of vegetables. It's about balance and variety. Next time we can go to take a tour of the street food. You have to know where to go though. My friend who came from Hollywood in February, they asked me to take them on a day for a tour of street food. The food is better on the street than in a five-star restaurant. The flavors are much better.

Cherizar: Is it better to cook food outside in the earth, in the dirt?

Miktlan: It has to do with the energy of the people, their love, their authenticity, or their anger. The factor of transference. If I put my hand here, I transmit a part of me on the wall. And if I take off my hand, my DNA is left on the wall. If you touch the food, you pass your DNA.

Cherizar: Why is it time to share your knowledge with the world?

Miktlan: Because we spent a long time with two cultures, and the European culture did not accept us. But now they are starting to accept it. So in 1989, we think that it was a moment where they could accept us.

Cherizar: Do you believe the knowledge is in our DNA and is being activated in this new age?

Miktlan: Yes, your DNA has information from our ancestors, not from reincarnations. The life we have in this moment is unique. But at the same moment, you collect all the information from your DNA. You have a father and mother, even if you don't know them, you have them. And they have a father and a mother, and that grows and grows. Fifty-two generations is a million persons. All of this information is in your body.

Cherizar: Do you believe in past lives?

Miktlan: No.

Cherizar: So what does it mean when you meet someone and it feels like you already know them?

Miktlan: There are two cases. This experience is one you have already had with someone else, but you are just not paying attention. Like when women marry someone like their father. The second case is the attraction is biological; the DNA profiles are complementary. The other person is your match.

Cherizar: Do you believe someone can be together forever?

Miktlan: If you are tied together, yes. If you are tied econom-ically or social status or business. They can stay together forever, but sometimes it's just habit. I know people who loved each other for a long time though. I remember one couple from my tradition, who were one hundred years old, and I saw them make their offerings together, and when they finished, they kissed each other and hugged and went to bed together. My parents are the same case. My father died, but my mother still loved him. She never paid atten-tion to anyone else and would remember him every day. I never saw them yell at each other or disrespect each other. Only one time I saw my mom disagree with my dad. It was the only time in my whole life. This is impressive.

Cherizar: Do you ever provide counsel for couples?

Miktlan: Yes, we have ceremonies for people to help them stay together. You can call it a wedding. We talk to them beforehand to see what their intentions are, but people do strange things in relationships. People can live better if they have a simple life and speak truthfully. If you want to be with someone else, you tell them. If you want to be with another couple, then you should say it. At the very begin-ning though, you have to speak the truth of what you want. I have a lawyer who only speaks the truth, and he always wins, even when his client is at fault.

I looked behind me through the window, and I could see the sun start its descent. As I turned back, Miktlan said it was time to build the fire for the temāzcalli. So he walked back to where we were earlier, where he had already laid out everything for the fire. There were some grasses, big and small sticks, and some porous rocks. As I watched him build the fire, I could see how every aspect of the temāzcalli was a part of the ritual, from choosing the sticks to build it with, to the animal hide to cover it with. And, of course, building the fire. Everything was a ritual. He spoke about the importance of each step as it happened. He built the fire in a very methodical way, and he prayed the entire time. Once the fire had started to get going, he began to walk around it and to speak in his native language. Then he said, "The fire is ours now."

As we waited for the fire to get hot enough, I started to prepare myself mentally for what I was about to do. I was scared, so I called my son on FaceTime. I had to see his smile before I did this. He was wearing a medal around his neck that he got after his first snowboarding lesson. Hugo had the biggest smile on his face, and I immediately felt calm. It was like when he was born, when his energy stopped me from shaking.

After I said goodbye to Hugo, Miktlan said he was ready to start. It was time for me to enter the womb of Mother Earth.

We stood outside the temāzcalli in the darkness, and he asked me to place my offering on the ground. I placed a necklace of white and rose quartz that I had around my neck, and he placed his necklace of blue skulls next to it. He said a prayer. I kept asking him what he was saying, and he kept telling me that he would tell me later. I took off my clothes and went inside, crouching and crawling in my blue bathing suit.

He told me that the ceremony would symbolize four phases: nature, instincts, willpower, and consciousness. He told me that if at any point I wanted to come out, to just tell him. I told myself that I wasn't coming out until the end; I had never felt so determined to get burned. Miktlan placed the first pile of rocks in the temāzcalli. The heat was inviting at first, so I invited it. But still, I kept myself as far away from the fire as I could. I knew that the heat had a bad side. I lay down on the dirt and closed my eyes, sinking into the earth and into the moment. My mind started to wander, and I saw my energy blend with the smoke drifting outside. The smoke cleansed me and carried my secrets into the starry, starry night.

Lying there in the dirt seemed to immediately connect me to a place I had never traveled to before. In this place, I could hear the distinctive sound of the African drum in the distance, and I could see a group of tribesmen and women gathered around a fire. They were dancing, and they were looking into the fire. And it was like through the fire, we could finally speak to each other and dance together again. I've always felt so disconnected from my roots because of slavery. I could never truly know where I came from. In that moment though, when I could just so much as smell my ancestors next to me, I knew that it was this experience now, and those before, and those that will come, that will teach me who I am. Doña Susana had told me that my roots were not cut, Miktlan had told me that everything was in my DNA, and my heart told me that I am the Cosmos. Nothing could truly separate me from my Nature.

Miktlan placed the second pile of rocks in the temāzcalli. It was starting to get really hot now, and I kept burying myself further in the earth. It was the only relief I had, the only protection. He put water on the rocks and the steam engulfed me, traveling from front to back. It was so hot that it burned my skin. I started to cry out in my head to my ancestors: "Please help me! Please guide me!" My first instinct was to scream out to Miktlan that it was too hot, and he needed to open it up, but instead, I just let it burn. I let it burn and let my mind get lost. I let go of my mind. My mind was getting in the way. My heart was calling out to me to dig deep now, so I did. I started to see everyone I had loved and lost around me. I saw my brother Yannick standing outside the tent, and my aunt Fatiha, and my grandmother Naomi. They were standing together for me. I started to pick up the dirt and rub it all over my body. I had to find the cold to match this heat. I had to overcome my need to flee or even fight; I had to remember that there is a third instinct, to freeze.

Miktlan placed the third pile of rocks in the temāzcalli. I was ready. I felt that it couldn't get any hotter than what I had already experienced. I had changed by now. The fire and I were friends now. I could talk to the fire and ask it to take it easy. I asked the fire to not burn my skin this time, and it didn't, but still I needed some air. I dug myself down further, to find any pockets of air that were hidden near the edge of the tent. Any relief I could find, I found. The ways to survive this came to me in my time of need, just as Miktlan had said: a gift of ancestral DNA. I could hear Miktlan chanting and saying prayers for me in the distance. I had asked him repeatedly to tell me what he was saying, and he wouldn't because he knew I would figure it out. He was praying for me to find the willpower to stay committed, the willpower that was within me. I found it everywhere then; in the fire that burned me and in the dirt that gave me relief, in the things that I resisted and in the things I was letting go. If willpower is courage and courage is from the heart, as the Leo in me would say, then it all leads back to love. Love had been the guiding force of this journey into my underworld, and now I see that the ending is the consciousness of love.

I could hear my heart beating as Miktlan placed the last pile of rocks in my tomb.

With all the love I had felt, with all the love I had strived to embody, I realized I fear losing it. I fear losing those whom I love. Perhaps it started with losing my brother and feeling that if only I had shown him more love, perhaps he would have felt it. Or maybe it was even earlier, when the man who I *knew* loved me, my father, abandoned me for a greater love of himself. And even so, as a mother, I never felt a fear more palpable, more tangible, than the fear of losing my son.

It is that and it is this; it is all of that—all of the aforementioned—that I must let go. I could feel the power of the temāzcalli will free me now, but what after that? How will I be able to let go again, when fear comes back? How will I stay beholden to this consciousness of love that I have found? I already felt it slipping away; I already felt it fleeing. And with this discovery, I needed to get out. It felt as if I had sailed a long way, across oceans of darkness, until finally the light of the moon lit up the sky, and I broke down in tears upon seeing such a sight, upon knowing that one mission had ended, and another one had begun.

I called out to Miktlan, and he came to help me crawl out. From my knees I stood, and he drenched me in cold water. He poured buckets and buckets of cold water over me. And he poured it again and again. I screamed. The cold was so shocking, but at the same time, so amazing. Perhaps no greater feeling than making it through. Perhaps no greater feeling than free.

We walked back into the house, and he showed me where the bathroom was. I looked at myself in the mirror and started to laugh. I had dirt all over my body and face, and the biggest smile on my face. I felt incredible. I took a shower and washed away all of the dirt, and I gave thanks to everyone who had joined me on my journey of life so far: my parents who had given me life, and the life I was able to create in a son. I gave thanks to the dirt of the Earth that was going down the drain, and I thanked the water that rushed over me. I thanked the mountains that stood next to me, and all the masters I had met. And I thanked Miktlan for being the one to guide me through my underworld. And then finally, I thanked me.

After the shower I sat down in front of Miktlan. I sat down in the room where we always sat. I could see how proud he was of me. He had the biggest smile, and he had that energy of pride for someone else. He asked me about my journey, and I told him everything that came to my mind. I told him about the things I did to survive. He told me that at some point he saw a shadow leave the tent. In my head I imagined a dark figure scrambling back into the darkness whence it came.

I thanked him then for praying for me and said that I had heard every word.

Two months later, on March 17, 2020, Miktlan Ehekateotl took his last breath. His words in this book represent his final message to the world. I will never forget how happy he was to see me make it through the darkness and be reborn. I can't believe he is no longer here. He seemed to have so much more life in him, but I guess he was older than I thought, or maybe it was just his time. I guess we all have a time that we are destined to die. He didn't tell me this in life, but now upon his death I have learned that *Mictlan* in Nahuatl means "place of the dead": the place in Aztec mythology where the deceased must go through in order to free their souls. I imagine him in the heavens learning to fly, so fierce and so free.

The New Shamanism

In all certainty it is the dark, not the light, that brings us together.

For years I was obsessed with true crime shows and the intricacies of detective work, but when Yannick was murdered, I couldn't have cared less about the criminal being caught. I understood then what finality truly was and the gaping hole that it leaves behind. There was nothing that could bring him back and no justice that could salve what was happening within me. Every relationship in my life splintered, and it breaks me to realize how much more than one life was lost. But in the end, there couldn't have been a better advisor to the light than the darkness I experienced that day. I felt abandoned, yes, but I also felt a vulnerability emerge from me that I used not just as a bridge to connection, but a pathway to creation.

The death of my marriage was a slow breaking of our shared heart, and that slowness gave us a soft place to fall. Even so, I was in a very fragile place when I met Emilio. I was mourning my marriage, and he was mourning his mom, who was dying in the hospital. So he and I were both in a dark place when we met, and perhaps that's why our light together seemed so bright. I felt so much for someone so fast, so the rejection was more excruciating than anything I'd ever felt. But it was the thing that finally broke me open. The true self that I'd always been searching for finally emerged in her wholeness. In her light and her dark, and in full embracement of the colossal waterfall of emotions that was her. It was as if every emotion I had hidden away in my life was revealed to the world. And it was only then that I could love, even without the expected reciprocity. It killed me, but it was true. The discovery of how much I could love a stranger was what opened the pathway to finally loving myself unconditionally.

And therein lay the Divine Feminine: in my darkest places. On the surface, I was studying indigenous culture, but beneath that, I was learning how to use darkness as a tool for spiritual alchemy. Death didn't just bring destruction; it brought the revelation of the type of healer I was meant to become. I was thriving in the midst of the chaos. It was as if I lived for it—not because I craved the dark, but because I was always able to transform it into the light. My ability to overcome, to remain risen in spite of insurmountable challenges, had started to define my very nature. Everything I was creating and expressing began to be birthed during my lowest moments. The moments where I would be bawling, screaming underwater, dancing, and writing for my life. Those were the moments I was reminded of my gift to transform pain into power.

It was then, in the midst of all that I was becoming, and right on the heels of my return from Ecuador, that I decided to host my first healing retreat. I called it "The Goddess Retreat." In my announcement, I said that it would be a day of "healing work in Nature . . . a day where we could remember who we truly are, and allow the Goddess within to emerge." I made the call, and the people came. It sold out in just a few days.

I'll never forget when the retreat was just starting, and the women were walking through the door one by one, getting cleansed by the smoke of palo santo. One of the women walked through, and as soon as she hugged me, she broke down in front of everyone and sobbed in my arms. The threshold that she passed through was a big one for her, and for all of us who were there to bear witness. And that was just the beginning of me witnessing the most beautiful forms of breaking down, the most beautiful displays of vulnerability. That's when I realized how critical this healing work was for all of us: the healers and those seeking to be healed. Vulnerability is a gift that we gave to each other.

Everything came together so effortlessly for my first healing retreat. All of the collaborators were already in my life, and we each had a unique skill that could be crafted into a beautiful offering for energetic transformation. I was convinced that this was exactly what I should be doing.

Once I returned home from Mexico City, the idea for my second retreat emerged as my identity as the alchemist came to life. And so I decided to use the very season we were inhabiting, the winter, as the source of our magic for this retreat. I called it "The Womb of Winter" because, after all, it was the winter that had made me. I logged onto my Instagram and recorded a story that began: "The winter offers us the greatest challenges, and with that, the greatest fuel for spiritual alchemy." I went on to talk about the story of Persephone and her journey into the underworld, marking the winter; and her rising back from that dark place, marking the beginnings of spring.

My identity as a writer was also taking hold, and I enjoyed offering the healing of my words and of the parables in my stories. I had also harnessed my power to intuitively encapsulate the collective energy so that I could see exactly the medicine that was needed and curate the offerings for the day. My form of medicine was not just understanding how to create an event and teach spiritual alchemy, but also to anchor the ritual of the Talking Circle. The Circle was always the center of the retreat, and the center of the magic for the day. And it was what I saw as the bridge from the ancient shamanism to the shamanism of the modern day. The Circle was our path back to the beginning, as well as a way for us to create connections with each other, binding ourselves as one.

I worked with three collaborators for the retreat, so that with all our gifts we could provide a more comprehensive form of chakra therapy, and most importantly, wisdom and guidance on how to embody our divinity so that we may connect with the ancient rituals and tools we have forgotten. So with our combined skill sets and the wisdom from the shamans, I wove a healing basket, so to speak.

Serena was "The Witch." She was the magician of movement and represented the element of water. I wove her gifts with those of Don Acho's, to construct an offering of yoga therapy at high noon (a portal of power) and an ecstatic dance therapy session at the end of the retreat. Ecstatic dance was the element that represented how Serena and I loved to lose ourselves through movement by letting go of all shame and any rules other than our own. It truly marked the birthing of the Goddess within in every circumstance that I witnessed. It was how we time-traveled to the time of the ancient temple priestess, conjuring with her hips, scantily clad.

Katherine was "The Scientist." She was the magician of the mind and represented the element of air. She was like Miktlan in the way that she healed through the power of our intelligence and our evidentiary experiences. Using this perspective, we grounded the retreat in a very nonmystical, scientific, modern way, by providing evidence of how spirituality is related to quantum physics, and how we should act as scientists by experimenting and gathering evidence of our healing and holistic health theories. Katherine brought the element of novelty by introducing us to something new that we never tried or heard of before.

Medusa was "The Oracle." She was the magician of mystic and represented the element of fire. She would open the circle by bridging us to our ancestors and to our future destinies simultaneously. She is a very gifted medium, so this was natural for her. At the time, she was actually my healer, whom I had found on Instagram. She used sound therapy, and her gifts were cultivated through the generations that came before her. She was like Don Shairy, seeing into the fire of our collective future.

I was "The Alchemist." I was the magician of matter and represented the element of earth. I connected most to Don Alberto's spirit and Doña Susana's ceremonial magic. On the morning of the retreat, it was my role to cultivate and transform the energy for our sacred container, the Circle, so that's what I did. I walked outside onto my front porch to connect with the trees that surrounded me and the mountain that I stood on. I could see more mountains in front of me, in the distance. I closed my eyes, but even with my eyes closed, I could see the sun dawning before me. I thought of Don Alberto traveling through the river and Miktlan walking through a field of dreams in the sky. I traveled to the subterranean caverns below the pyramids of Teotihuacán, to see the crystallized globes that are hidden down there. Then I traveled to a place I had gone to during a hypnosis session, which was underground as well. It was like the library of Atlantis connected to the ancient pyramids in Egypt. I traveled back in actual time next, to the moment I first heard the word *shaman*. I was standing in my old house listening to my roommate tell a story about how he had died and come back to life. And then I went to Ecuador to hear Don Acho tell me that Ayahuasca used to be taken by the master shamans only on every equinox, and that's how they would time travel. I started to have all these thoughts and memories simultaneously.

I thought about how I used to be obsessed with the idea of 73 percent of energy being "dark energy." I took a deep breath, and I could see God creating the Earth from the dark waters, as I sat on a white chair on my front porch. It was the dead of winter, but I could hear the fire crackling beside me. Everything converged from all sides, and I was who and where I was meant to be. I knew that the time for the Goddess was now. Four shamans, four elements, and four directions.

I realized that the magic of bringing women together and binding them as one was so powerful that it could not be contained.

So we started to gather at every new or full moon to host healing circles. This routine started a very visible movement in Montréal, and with social media, I could see this wave of new shamanism emerging across the globe. It seemed to me that we were collectively traveling back to the time when the Goddess was worshipped, before patriarchy plundered and darkness fell. The Circle not only connected us to an ancient knowledge we had lost but also allowed for us, as healers, to also be healed through its power. This was something I did not expect. It was then that I realized something was truly shifting in the world. I knew it was the Divine Feminine rising that was bringing about this global balancing, but I had no clue what events this great change would bring about . . . until, in February 2020, the Canadian government announced that all flights from Montréal were grounded. I'll never forget reading this headline.

I knew then that this was it. This is the darkness that would precede the light of a new day. The end of the world as we knew it was upon us. And with that, a chance to create Utopia. We already have the tools—that I am convinced of. We just have to remember how. This will be the age when we remember how and when we remember who we truly are.

I am someone who would walk straight into the unknown, into the darkest valley, just for the chance to feel the warmth of the sun again, after a winter I thought would never end. I am also someone who would drive across the country from sea to shining sea, with my ex-husband and my son. On a journey where we would imagine ourselves as the people who won the West. And although there would be many rocks and thorns on our journey westward we would be triumphant, as we are now, as a family. Always as a family. Our reality is a future we never imagined, but it was the future we needed most to heal our past. As Jack Kerouac says in *On the Road*: "We had finally found the magic land at the end of the road and we never dreamed the extent of the magic." We've made it to the place where we are the children of the sun again, but the question remains: Will we all make it?

When I ponder this question, I think back to when I was young, to a memory of me standing on the beach watching Yannick float away in the ocean, in complete surrender. He seemed to be so at peace.

Swallow us whole, great ocean, and bring us to your golden shores! Ahooooo!

Acknowledgments

To Hugo:

Thank you for incessantly asking me when this book would be published. Every word was inspired by my love for you. You have given me more life than I could ever give you. I love you!

To Bruno:

Thank you for always encouraging and supporting me in all my pursuits. Without you, I would have never discovered my passion for writing and traveling. Thank you for walking beside me in this life.

To my parents, Valerie and Matt:

Thank you for giving me the confidence and encouragement to know that I could be capable of anything. Thank you for letting me go to pursue my dreams across the country and across the world. I also want to thank you, Mama, for giving me the belief and the strength in my relationship with God.

To Yannick:

Thank you for saving me when I was a little girl, and for giving me the power to confront the greatest pain in losing you. I miss you so much. I will cherish our memories together, forever.

To my father, Wayne:

I'll never forget the first time I read your screenplay and felt the desire to write something of my own one day. I love that we have this in common.

To Shari Reinhart:

Thank you for helping me to write what I was meant to.

To Grace and Randy:

Thank you for helping me transform my manuscript into a book that I am incredibly proud of!

To Petrona Joseph:

Thank you for your generosity as a PR consultant, and as my dear friend.

To my soul family:

To all my friends who have supported me on this journey, and to all my readers, thank you!

Lastly, to the Most High and all my spirit guides: thank you for showing me the way!

About the Author

Cherizar Walker is a researcher and storyteller who lives a life of multifaceted pursuits. She was born and raised in Los Angeles, where she began a successful career in aerospace engineering. In 2013, she decided to follow her heart to Montréal, where her passion for the integrative nature of writing and the healing arts ignited. This led her to receiving her shamanic healing certification from the Andean Masters in 2019, and to discovering her higher purpose in life. *The Conception of Utopia* is her first book.